CHAKRAS

An Hachette UK Company
www.hachette.co.uk

First published in Great Britain in 2021 by
Godsfield, an imprint of
Octopus Publishing Group Ltd
Carmelite House
50 Victoria Embankment
London EC4Y 0DZ
www.octopusbooks.co.uk
www.octopusbooksusa.com

Distributed in the US by
Hachette Book Group
1290 Avenue of the Americas
4th and 5th Floors
New York, NY 10104

Distributed in Canada by
Canadian Manda Group
664 Annette St.
Toronto, Ontario, Canada M6S 2C8

Thimela A. Garcia asserts the moral right to be
identified as the author of this work.

ISBN 978-1-84181-500-8

A CIP catalogue record for this book is available
from the British Library.

Printed and bound in China

10 9 8 7 6 5 4 3 2

All reasonable care has been taken in the
preparation of this book but the information
it contains is not intended to take the place of
treatment by a qualified medical practitioner.
Before making any changes in your health
regime, always consult a doctor. While all the
therapies detailed in this book are completely
safe if done correctly, you must seek
professional advice if you are in any doubt
about any medical condition. Any application
of the ideas and information contained in this
book is at the reader's sole discretion and risk.

Publishing Director: Stephanie Jackson
Commissioning Editor: Natalie Bradley
Art Director: Yasia Williams-Leedham
Senior Production Controller: Emily Noto

Project Editor: Clare Churly
Copy-editor: Mandy Greenfield
Designer: Leonardo Collina
Illustrator: Emilia Franchini

CHAKRAS

THE GUIDE TO PRINCIPLES, PRACTICES AND MORE

Thimela A. Garcia

Contents

Preface

My first encounter with the chakra system and energy healing dates back to my adolescent years, watching my mum doing different types of spiritual and holistic healing activities at home. I grew up in Latin America in a very spiritual environment, surrounded by crystals, candles, Tarot cards, incense sticks, saint figurines and an altar. There were mantras, meditation, herbal medicine, spiritual gatherings and white witchcraft – to name just a few of the techniques.

I still remember feeling a bit embarrassed about bringing my school friends over, for fear of being labelled a *bruja* ("witch" in Spanish). This was at the end of the 1980s and into the 1990s and in those days, especially in Latin America, not much was said about alternative medicine, even though it was already being studied and practised.

As a teenager, when I suffered from very bad stomach pains, my mum used to give me herbal teas and would place a yellow crystal on my abdomen, hovering her hands over it and chanting. I remember feeling a lot better afterwards: my mother's love, combined with this *medicina*, was a type of healing that stayed with me. My mother was the person who introduced me to the word "chakra". She would go around the house smudging herbs and reciting prayers, followed by a chakra visualization meditation. Little did I know at the time that I would follow in her footsteps – and write a book on chakras 30 years later!

I am passionate about chakras, and I feel it is my duty and my responsibility as a holistic practitioner to educate and inform the public about the great benefits of energy healing. There were not many books about these topics when I was learning about them; energy healing was still quite a niche practice. I am pleased to see that we are now moving in the right direction, toward a more natural and holistic approach to wellness.

In this book you will learn about the chakras and how they affect our physical, emotional and spiritual wellbeing. I hope the book's simply approach will enable you to understand your chakra system clearly and to identify easily whether your chakras are blocked, open, overactive or underactive, and learn how to balance them for optimum health.

Each chakra relates to a different area of your life. You will learn how to work with each one to create the life you want. Working with your chakras gives you insight into which areas of your life need the most work in order to be energetically balanced. You will find tools and techniques to open, clean and bring your chakras back into balance, so that you can enjoy a happier and healthier life.

Before we get started, I would like to take this opportunity to congratulate you on claiming ownership of your own health, and on taking the first step on a colourful and empowering journey. Remember that knowledge is power; and the more you understand about your body and its functionality, the better choices you will make toward a joyful, healthy and meaningful life.

Thimela A. Garcia

1

WHAT ARE CHAKRAS?

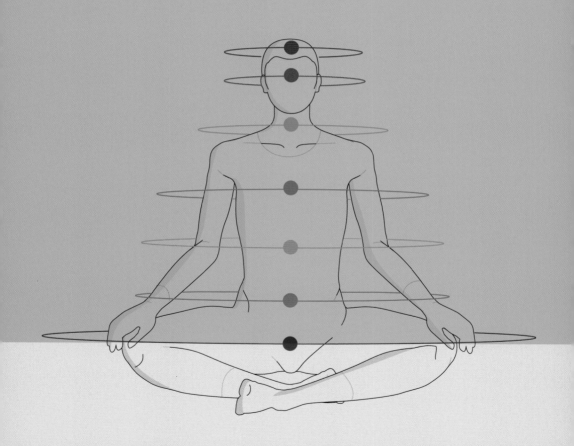

Introduction to the Chakras

The chakras are vortices of energy – they are the energy centres in your body. The Sanskrit word *chakra* means "wheel", and the human body has 114 chakras or energy centres. However, the most important ones are the seven main chakras that are located in the centre of the body, running from the top of the head to the base of the spine. These are known as the primary or main chakras because they have a direct influence on the physical body and are the chakras that have been studied the most.

Starting from the base, these seven chakras are: the Muladhara or root chakra; the Svadhisthana or sacral chakra; the Manipura or solar plexus chakra; the Anahata or heart chakra; the Vishuddha or throat chakra; the Ajna or third eye chakra and the Sahasrara or crown chakra. Other chakras are more related to the spiritual realm and we don't know as much about them, because our level of consciousness is conditioned to the physical realm of our three-dimensional existence.

The seven main chakras are positioned in a perfect straight line in the middle of our bodies and relate to the body systems and key organs. When they are balanced and open, they can help to boost your immune system. These wheels of energy are not present on a physical level, but in the astral or spiritual level and, more specifically, in the subtle (emotional) body. Chakras have a strong relationship with our spiritual, mental and emotional states of being, and this is why it is important to look after your chakras and keep them balanced.

I view the chakras as little internal doors that allow universal energy to enter and communicate between the physical and subtle bodies. Chakra energy spins in a clockwise direction as it moves the energy out of our body into the energy field around us. It spins anticlockwise to pull in energy from the area around us, and from other people and situations around us. The chakras are constantly spinning these energies, so when there is a blockage in any of the chakras, it stops the free flow of energy and causes the chakras to become unbalanced.

You can think of chakras as receptors and emitters of universal-energy information. However, sometimes we may experience inconvenience when one or more of these receptors stops working properly. It is essential for the optimum functionality of the chakras that they are cleaned and, most importantly, that they are balanced and perfectly aligned with the rest of the chakras. This means that the energy of one of these chakras should not be vibrating excessively high (overactive) in relation to the rest of the chakras, nor should it be vibrating too low (underactive). Chakras can be open or closed, active or underactive, depending on how well *prana*, or life-force energy, is able to flow through them. The goal is to keep the seven main chakras equally open, so that there is an optimum flow of energy and balance.

The Purpose of Chakras

All of the seven chakras are important, and they are interconnected with each other. Usually balancing one chakra will affect another chakra. The vital energy that the chakras transmit is known as *prana*, ki or chi – it's the life force and is a particular energy that identifies each person.

The chakras are receptors of energy that comes from the Sun, the universe and the Source (also known as the divine or God), and these energies are channelled to us through our Higher Self: this is usually described as that part of yourself that is unlimited, eternal, omnipotent and a conscious intelligence within your being. The Higher Self is your soul or Atman (the Sanskrit term for the soul or the true self) and serves as a bridge or portal to connect us to these universal spiritual energies. Despite the Higher Self being within ourselves, it sits in the higher realms and not in the physical realm, and this is why in order to access it and connect to our Higher Self, we must detach from the outer world and connect to the inner world. This can be done through meditation: by bringing calmness and stillness into us.

The chakras are so important because they transform and process all these energies and distribute them across the systems in our internal body. The seven principal chakras are in complete harmony with the energies of the higher realms and form the interconnection between the energy body (see page 36) and the physical body through the main endocrine glands, which secrete hormones into the bloodstream. The chakras convey energy to all our internal body systems, such as the nervous system, the endocrine system and the digestive system, to mention just a few.

Our seven main chakras serve different purposes in the body. Each chakra is associated with a different set of organs and systems, with one of the nine endocrine glands and with a group of nerves, making them important elements in healing. The chakras work in two ways:

- **Internally**: moving up and down the body, and over the physical organs where the chakras are located.
- **Externally**: producing and radiating energy that makes up our electromagnetic field, or aura. This electromagnetic field can extend for about an arm's length around the body. It has seven layers, each of which is related to the physical, mental, emotional and spiritual conditions of human beings.

Chakras of Matter and Spirit

It is important to call the chakras by their original Sanskrit names because the sound of the name, together with the intention, resonates with the vibration of each particular chakra. Each sound that we emit is a vibrational note of big power.

The three lower chakras from the base of the spine to the abdomen – also known as the "lower-triangle chakras" – are the chakras of matter; they are associated with the unconscious and are where past traumas, and even past-life experiences, are imprinted. They are physical in nature and are related to the lower-self, physical and material world. They are Muladhara (the root chakra), Svadhisthana (the sacral chakra) and Manipura (the solar plexus chakra).

The three upper chakras, from the throat to the top of the head, are the chakras of Spirit. They are related to our connection with the spiritual world, the divine and consciousness. These are the chakras connected to our Higher Self. They are Vishuddha (the throat chakra), Ajna (the third eye chakra) and Sahasrara (the crown chakra).

Anahata (the heart chakra), which is located at the heart centre, lies at the middle of the seven chakras and balances the energies of the three lower chakras of matter and the three upper chakras of Spirit. Anahata is a spiritual chakra, but it also connects and unites the mind, body and soul energies. This chakra deals with both Lower Self and Higher Self energies: it is where the unconscious and the conscious meet. Living our lives with a blocked Anahata can considerably impact on both our physical and energy bodies.

Many spiritual systems include other minor chakras throughout the body. For instance, the Lalana Chakra is situated at the base of the mouth and is associated with Vishuddha. In some Shaivist traditions (made up of those who worship the god Shiva) there are 114 chakras, and 112 of these are present inside the body.

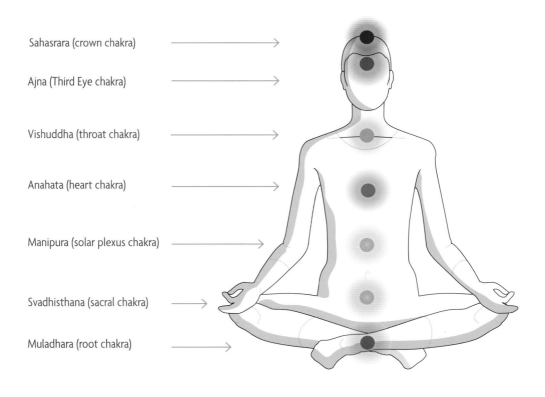

Sahasrara (crown chakra)

Ajna (Third Eye chakra)

Vishuddha (throat chakra)

Anahata (heart chakra)

Manipura (solar plexus chakra)

Svadhisthana (sacral chakra)

Muladhara (root chakra)

"I am ready to transform my life. I am prepared to take the first step on a journey of knowledge, ancient wisdom and empowerment."

The History of Chakras

In the early centuries of the first millennium BCE, two distinct cultures existed in India: Vedic and non-Vedic. The Vedas were sacred texts that revealed what was heard from the higher source, and they are believed to be the oldest scriptural texts of the Hindu faith. The non-Vedic culture comprised Jainism and Buddhism, which didn't accept the authority of the Vedas and, as a result, evolved as two separate faiths.

There are records showing that the chakra system originated in India in the early traditions of Hinduism between 1500 and 500 BCE. It is referred to in the Vedas (this term comes from a Sanskrit word meaning "knowledge" or "wisdom"), but it is also believed that this knowledge was passed down through oral tradition, usually from a guru to his students. It was handed down orally for thousands of years before being codified by the sage known as Patanjali in his *Yoga Sutras*, several centuries before Christ. Records show that the word "chakra" first appeared within the Hindu Vedas, but not meaning a psychic energy centre, as we know it today.

According to the American Indologist David Gordon White, the chakras were introduced in about the 8th century CE in Buddhist texts as inner energy centres, and these medieval texts mentioned four chakras, while later Hindu texts mentioned or added more. However, in contrast to Gordon White, Georg Feuerstein – a German Indologist specializing in the philosophy of yoga – states that early Hindu texts do mention "*cakras*" as psychospiritual vortices, along with other terms found in Tantra, such as *prana* and *nadi*. Tantra is the mystical or esoteric side of Hindu or Buddhist traditions that probably co-developed around the middle of the 1st millennium CE. In Sanskrit the word *Tantra* means "loom", "warp" or "weave"; in the Indian traditions it means "text", "method", "technique" or "practice". Chakras were originally meditation points that were often visualized as a lotus flower or a disc containing a particular deity (god or goddess) used in Tantric tradition. Therefore we could say that the chakra system we know today has its origins in occult and mystical Tantric practices. The earliest texts related to Tantric practice date from around 600 CE. By the 10th century an extensive manuscript existed.

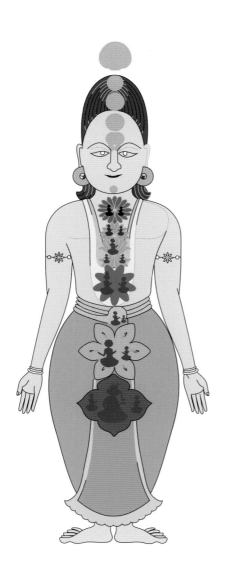

Chakras are part of esoteric medieval-era beliefs, and are thought of as both physiological and psychic centres that emerged across Indian traditions. It was believed that human life existed in two parallel dimensions: one was the physical body (the mass body), and the other was the physiological, emotional body (the subtle body); the latter was made up of *nadis*, or energy channels, that were connected to the chakras. Some of the beliefs even suggested that the human body consisted of 88,000 chakras, although this figure varied, depending on the different traditions.

The important chakras are stated in both Hindu and Buddhist texts, and were arranged in a line along the spinal cord, from the base of the spine to the top of the head. The Tantric traditions worked on the chakras using different breathing techniques and meditation, with the guidance of a guru.

Different Interpretations and Systems

When you read about the origins of the chakra system you will find that it is a wide, still largely unexplored world and we are really only scratching the surface of it now. The chakra system that we know today is a version that has resulted from Western influence and from different translations of the original ancient texts.

Over the years, the chakras have seized the Western imagination, but we should realize that earlier works of Western occultism adopted the Sanskrit terms without really understanding them. The more you research the history of the chakras, the more contradictions and discrepancies you may find, depending on the yoga lineage, the schools and culture in question, and so on. Sometimes the concepts lie far away from their true chakra history and Indian sources.

Many Buddhist texts, for example, refer to five chakras, whereas Hindu sources offer six or seven. The number of major chakras varied between the different traditions, but typically ranged between four and seven. In Indian traditions there are references to a life force within our bodies that is identified as *prana*, whereas in Japan *ki* and in Chinese tradition *chi* was believed to be the universal life force that is present in all matter. Two polar forces were also recognized: the masculine energy and feminine energy, or yin and yang. When these two forces were in balance, people were considered to be healthy and happy.

Everything that exists in our universe is made up of energy: all matter is, at its core, composed of atoms, and atoms are constituted by electromagnetic charge – so in reality everything that exists is a manifestation of energy. We are exposed to, and in constant interaction with, different forms of energy.

The life force, or *prana*, is the essential energy that keeps the human body animated; and when that energy is not present, the body dies. *Prana* keeps us alive and in motion. *Prana* flows within our body through the energy channels or pathways known as *nadis*, and these are responsible for maintaining the functionality of the body's cellular activity. When trapped or blocked *prana* is present within us, it can manifest as stiffness of the body and a subsequent accumulation of toxins. When there is a free flow of *prana*, toxins are removed from the system, enabling the life force to reach all parts of the body freely. As a result there is good health.

The most commonly studied chakra system describes six major chakras, plus a seventh centre that is not always regarded as one. This is what I learned from my guru, and from Kundalini teachers during my teacher-training yoga course in India. According to Gavin Flood, a British scholar who specializes in Shaivism and phenomenology and has an interest in South Asian traditions, this system of six chakras first appeared in the Kubjikamata Tantra, an 11th-century Kaula work (Kaula being a religious tradition in Shaktism and Tantric Shaivism that is characterized by rituals and symbolism to worship the goddess Shakti). The chakras in Tantric tradition were originally considered meditation aids. The yogi (yoga expert), or aspiring yogi, progressed in meditation practice from the lower chakras to the highest chakras, blossoming in Sahasrara, and this was also referred as the path of spiritual journey.

Both Hindu and Buddhist texts also refer to a dormant energy at the lowest chakra which, once awakened, flows through the Sushumna *nadi*, piercing the chakras until it arrives at Sahasrara. In Hindu texts this energy is known as Kundalini; and in Buddhists texts it is called Candali or Tummo.

Modern Influences

Rudolf J Lorenz Steiner, an Austrian philosopher of the 19th and early 20th centuries, considered the chakra system to be dynamic and to be evolving with new generations. He suggested that this system was different for modern people than it was in ancient times, and that it will continue changing and evolving in future times. Steiner also suggested how to develop the chakras by various methods, such as thoughts, the will and feelings.

In 1918 Sir John Woodroffe (also known as Arthur Avalon) introduced to the West the Shakta theory of the seven main chakras in his book *The Serpent Power*. This was a translation of 11th-century Kaula work, the two Indian texts the *Satcakra-nirupana* and the *Paduka-Pancaka*, and showed the chakra system in grand detail and complexity. Later the idea of the chakras was adopted into a more Western version by C W Leadbeater in his book *The Chakras*, which was influenced by other scholars and authors interested in this topic, such as Johann Georg Gichtel (a disciple of the philosopher Jakob Böhme) and his book *Theosophia practica*, which was published in 1696. In his work Gichtel directly referred to the inner-force centres – the chakras.

The New Age is a term applied to a range of spiritual and religious beliefs and practices that grew rapidly in the Western world in the 1970s. During this period the chakras were thought to vitalize the physical body, and to be associated with the physical, mental and emotional bodies. They were considered to be centres for the life force, or *prana*, that flows through the pathways called *nadis*. New Age practices often associate each different chakra with certain colours. In various traditions, chakras are also associated with different physiological functions, and with different aspects of consciousness and of our lives. Some traditions visualize the chakras as lotus flowers.

Another contributor to this subject was the American author Anodea Judith, who wrote *Wheels of Life: A User's Guide to the Chakra System* in 1987, which sold thousands of copies. She is best known for reviving the chakra system of ancient yoga in the West.

And in 1996 the American author Caroline Myss published *Anatomy of the Spirit*, in which she stated that every experience of our life gets filtered through the chakra databases, and each event is recorded in the body's cells. She also described the chakras as being aligned in an ascending column from the base of the spine to the top of the head.

Although chakras are referred to as energy centres that reside in the psyche, modern authors such as Gary Osborn call the chakras metaphysical counterparts to the endocrine glands, and this is also supported by Anodea Judith's views. Other authors link the chakras with the nervous system, and Muladhara and Ajna with the pineal gland. During the New Age a novel version of the chakras was introduced, representing Newtonian colours that were unknown when these systems were originally created.

An Evolving Tradition

Chakras have evolved over the years, and I believe this evolution is essential, both for our own benefit and for the planet. There is now more research being undertaken into the chakra system and the subtle body, and we are using this incredible system more and more in modern times. As much as I am an advocate of keeping things closely to their tradition and real essence, I also appreciate that we live in a very different world from our ancestors. We face other types of challenges today, and if we can use the traditional system in a upgraded version to better suit our needs, then I think that is valid. As long as we are using all this wonderful knowledge given by our ancestors with an open mind and a positive approach, then we are doing what we are supposed to do. All the wisdom, ancient rules, texts and principles form a great base for us and will continue to guide us in becoming better, healthier and happier human beings. The same thing has happened with yoga, in terms of traditional yoga versus modern types. Both are excellent practices and are beneficial for mind, body and soul. I studied traditional Kundalini yoga, although sometimes I like to jazz up my practice with some of the *kriyas* taught by the spiritual teacher Yogi Bhajan. In Sanskrit the word *kriya* means "action" or "effort" and commonly referred to a completed action or practice within a yoga discipline, carried out to achieved a specific result.

We need the basic and traditional structure of the chakras, and we also need the new modern version of the chakra system, with its colours, musical notes, related organs and endocrine glands. Both systems empower us to be in control of our own wellbeing. We now relate better to the chakras, and it has never been so important as it is right now to understand that healing starts from the inside. We need to turn our attention to what is happening inside our bodies before we start applying hot compresses and taking painkillers without even trying to find the root of the problem.

Such high-profile alternative-medicine advocates as Deepak Chopra have popularized traditional healing systems in the West, such as balancing the chakras, which is believed to promote general wellbeing by ensuring the free flow of vital energy throughout the physical body. Although his concept of healing mind, body and soul through meditation remains unchanged, his approach has altered and evolved in line with the needs and modern times of new generations.

What Is Chakra Healing?

Before we dive into this topic, let me just say that chakra healing is easier than most people think. In fact you can carry out effective chakra healing at home or at your workplace – all you need is a few minutes of your time and true intent. The art of chakra healing has been used for centuries to balance the energy centres in the body. You can use a number of different methods and tools, such as crystals, energy healing or meditation, to achieve this. The end result will be a balanced, healthier body and a happier, more peaceful you.

The seven primary chakras correspond to vital areas of our mind, body and Spirit. Each chakra has its own colour, vibrational frequency and symbol. For example, the first chakra is found at the base of the spine and is known as Muladhara; it governs the spinal column, kidneys, legs, feet, rectum and immune system. When this chakra is out of balance, it may lead to physical and emotional ailments such as lower back pain, varicose veins, leg cramps, rectal conditions, depression and immune-related disorders. A lack of balance in Muladhara may be caused by feelings of low self-esteem, insecurity or family concerns.

Each energy centre must be vibrating at the proper frequency, independent of one another, in order for the entire body to vibrate in harmony. Therefore each chakra is equally important to the optimal functioning of the body, according to the chakra-healing tradition. Many powerful tools can affect the vibration of the chakras, and this is where "chakra balancing" comes into play. Chakra healing is all about bringing the vibration of each chakra back to its original vibrational frequency and obtaining a balanced chakra system that is able to deal not only with the energies within the body, but also with the energies around us.

Yoga, energy healing, crystals, music, *mudras* (hand positions), mantras (repeated sounds or words) and meditation bring the frequency of the chakras back into proper vibrational alignment. For example, Muladhara is represented by the colour red, so it will be greatly affected by crystals of this colour, such as red jasper, ruby or garnet. It is also affected by black stones, like onyx and black tourmaline, because of their earthy tone. During chakra healing a practitioner may use one or all of these stones to cleanse your Muladhara and bring it into harmony. Crystals have their own vibrational frequency and, based on their natural colour, can be matched to a specific chakra.

Chakra Meditation

Chakra meditation may also be used to open up your chakra centres and improve the flow of positive life-force energy in your body. During meditation you simply concentrate on each of the chakras in turn, starting with Muladhara and working your way up to Sahasrara. By imagining the flow of energy from chakra to chakra and their colours, you are helping to remove blockages in each energy centre that might be causing pain and disease.

I find this method of chakra healing particularly effective; it is one of my favourites to do in the morning after my yoga and breathwork practice. Meditating while balancing the chakras is a great way to achieve two things at once: a state of calm and a healthy energy flow. Practising yoga postures is also a good way to balance your chakras. An *asana* (yoga posture) that I love doing in my yoga practice is Ushtrasana, the Camel Pose, because of the great benefits it offers on a physical, mental and spiritual level. Despite being a backbend posture, it is in fact a chest-opener pose – it stretches the entire front of the body, the ankles, thighs, groin, spine and shoulders; it stimulates the digestive system, the nervous system and the adrenals. This posture opens the chest and is beneficial for respiratory conditions and for flexibility of the spine.

On the spiritual level, Ushtrasana opens up the solar plexus chakra, the heart chakra and the throat chakra, and doing few repetitions of this pose and holding it for few breaths while bringing awareness to those chakras can be very powerful – and sometimes even emotional. As this posture opens up the chakras, any trapped energy and emotional blockages are released, sometimes manifesting an overwhelming emotion.

Because the chakras govern every organ and system in your body, chakra healing has far-reaching health benefits. Chakra balancing can lead to improved heart, lung and brain health, better immunity and digestion, and may also help with depression, anxiety and other emotional imbalances. Many people believe that chakras have the power to transform your life both physically and spiritually. It is only when our chakras are in sync that we can truly access higher levels of consciousness and have a joyful, healthy life.

Vibrational Frequencies

Each chakra has its own vibrational frequency, due to its colour, its position in the body and its function. The lower the chakra, the denser and lower its frequency – for example, Muladhara is the lowest energy centre of the seven chakras and has a lower frequency than Sahasrara. The former is related to the material world and is associated with the Earth element, whereas the latter's high-vibrational frequency resonates with high levels of consciousness, connecting it to the spiritual realm and associating it with the Spirit element.

Because each chakra has its own vibrational frequency, it responds to a particular musical note whose frequency resonates with that specific chakra. We can translate the colour of a chakra into a musical note and frequency. There has been a lot of research into this over the years, and numerous studies support this theory. The colours associated with the chakras are also a form of energy, because colour is simply energy expressed as a light wavelength; sound is another form of energy vibrating at different wavelengths.

In the major Romance and Slavic languages, the syllables Do, Re, Mi, Fa, Sol, La and Ti are used to name notes in the same way that the letters C, D, E, F, G, A and B are used to name notes in English. *Solfeggio*, or *solfège*, is a method of naming pitches. It

Chakra	Syllable	Musical Note	Frequency
Muladhara	Do	C	396 Hz
Svadhisthana	Re	D	417 Hz
Manipura	Mi	E	528 Hz
Anahata	Fa	F	639 Hz
Vishuddha	Sol	G	741 Hz
Ajna	La	A	852 Hz
Sahasrara	Ti	B	963 Hz

works by assigning a syllable to each note of the musical scale. So rather than saying C, D, E, and so on, you can say Do, Re, Mi, etc.

So if we could hear with our ears the sound of the chakras as they are constantly flowing *prana* up and down in our body, it would be something like this: Do, Re, Mi, Fa, Sol, La, Ti, Ti, La, Sol, Fa, Mi, Re, Do, Do, Re, Mi, Fa, Sol, La, Ti... and so on. This is the sound of the chakra system in our body, together with the related frequency of that musical note.

This is pure harmony in our bodies: the miracle of creation and manifestation in ourselves. We are as incredible as the universe because we are a small form of the manifestation of the universe. Our bodies have been perfectly designed in accordance with this pure consciousness. And this is the beauty that we can see when we allow ourselves to understand our bodies beyond the physical form. We are beings made of energy and sound, we are vibration, and we are vibrating at a certain frequency that resonates with the vibrations around us and in the universe. The universe itself is vibration – it's constantly pulsing, expanding and contracting – and the energies around us are swirling and spinning, interconnecting with each other.

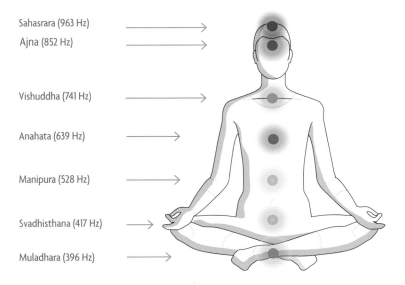

Sahasrara (963 Hz)

Ajna (852 Hz)

Vishuddha (741 Hz)

Anahata (639 Hz)

Manipura (528 Hz)

Svadhisthana (417 Hz)

Muladhara (396 Hz)

Using Mantras

A mantra is a healing power that originates from the human voice, and that can encourage and improve the body's natural healing abilities. Each chakra has its own *bija* (seed) mantra or sound, which, when chanted repeatedly and with intent, can clear emotional blockages and release negative energy, bringing balance to our bodies. In yogic tradition, mantras are used during meditation to achieve a meditative state, which promotes healing on many different levels: emotional, physical, mental and spiritual.

The mantras for the seven main chakras are:
* Muladhara = LAM
* Svadhisthana = VAM
* Manipura = RAM
* Anahata = YAM
* Vishuddha = HAM
* Ajna = OM
* Sahasrara = OM

In Pursuit of Chakra Healing

As well as employing the powerful art of chakra healing by yourself at home, I would highly recommend a visit to an experienced energy healer or Reiki practitioner, who will ask you plenty of questions about your health in order to pinpoint which of your chakras are most blocked or unbalanced. From there, they may employ any number of tools to help lead your energy centres into harmonious vibration.

Our chakras come out of balance easily and constantly, due to our fast pace and stressful way of living. In the same way that you avoid doing something that can potentially harm your physical body, so you should avoid doing something that could impact negatively on your chakras, because such imbalances in your chakras will manifest in your physical body later on. Remember that healing comes from the inside out. The wellbeing of your physical body strongly depends on how healthy your energy centres are.

All your lovely chakra-healing work will be lost if you go back to your former negative habits. For instance, let's say that you did a lovely chakra balance in the morning before going to work and are feeling peaceful and calm; however, on your way to work you allow the chaos of the busy roads, loud traffic, angry drivers, transport delays and so on to affect you and therefore to disturb your inner peace. Soon you will find yourself yelling at people or having negative thoughts, and by responding in this way you have brought imbalance back into your entire system – and by this I mean imbalance in your mind, body and soul. This can then manifest as headaches, shortness of breath, poor oxygen levels, raised blood pressure, ulcers, negative emotions and a poor state of mind… and the list goes on. Awareness in both our physical body and the subtle body is key!

Chakra healing is about bringing awareness into the energy centres and harnessing their beautiful qualities by actively practising what they stand for. The more you practise unconditional love, kindness, forgiveness and gratitude toward yourself and others, the more you are constantly raising the vibration of Anahata. By doing this, you are also unblocking and opening this chakra, inviting healing into it. To me, chakra healing isn't simply about lying down with crystals or meditating on each chakra; it is also about embracing the chakras, living our lives through the chakras and embodying their beautiful energies.

Morning Ritual

There are different rituals that you can do at home to heal the chakras and either prepare yourself for the day ahead or get ready – mentally, physically and emotionally – for bedtime and sleep. This is a morning ritual to do first thing in the day, so that you are refreshed and ready to face the day ahead. Practising this meditation regularly will set the tone for your day and will give you a more positive mindset. This morning ritual not only opens up the chakras so that you start the day with a balanced mind, body and soul, but also protects your energy field from negative and lower energies around you.

Duration: 15 minutes

1. Find a quiet space where you know you won't be interrupted. You can play nice relaxing, healing music, if you wish. Sit in a comfortable position on a chair or with crossed legs on the floor. Roll your shoulders back, and straighten your back so that it's nice and tall, but not stiff. Slightly tuck in your chin, so that you create a nice space at the back of your neck.

2. Rest your hands with your palms facing down on your knees. Close your eyes. Take a nice deep breath in through your nose, then breathe out through your mouth. Repeat this three times. Bring awareness to your body, from head to toes and then from toes to head.

3. Starting with Muladhara, bring awareness to the base of your spine and imagine a red light expanding, as you breathe in and out into this area. Take a nice deep inhale through your nose and, as you exhale, chant the mantra LAM. Repeat this mantra seven times before moving to the next chakra.

4. Svadhisthana is located below the navel area. Take a few deep inhalations, visualizing the colour orange expanding. When you are ready, breathe in and, as you exhale, chant nice and loud the mantra VAM. Chant this seven times.

5. Move on to Manipura, breathing in and out into your navel centre and imagining a bright-yellow light expanding as you inhale and exhale. As with the other two chakras, start chanting the sacred sound RAM loud enough that you can feel the vibration in the solar plexus of your body. Continue chanting this seven times.

6. Move on to Anahata. This time imagine a light forest-green growing and expanding, and use your breath to tap into the chakra of love and compassion. Chant the mantra YAM, just as you did with the other chakras. Continue with this seven times, then move to the next chakra.

7. Bring your awareness to Vishuddha, taking deep inhalations and exhalations through your nose and visualizing a light-blue colour getting bigger and bigger, illuminating the throat area of your body. Take a nice breath in and, as you breathe out, chant the sound HAM, which should be felt in your throat. Keep doing this for seven repetitions.

8. When you are ready, move on to Ajna. Bring awareness to your forehead between the eyebrows (the third eye), then take a few inhalations and exhalations as you tap into this chakra of wisdom and vision. When you are ready, chant the sound OM, focusing on that area. Still with your eyes closed, imagine a bright indigo-blue colour expanding as far as the radiation wishes to go. Stay here for seven chants before moving on.

9. Bring your awareness to Sahasrara at the top of your head and, as you breathe in and out, imagine a bright-violet light expanding from the top of your head and above it, like a flower opening and flourishing. Continue doing this and, when you are ready, begin to chant the sound OM. Stay here chanting this mantra seven times.

10. Once you have finished, still keeping your eyes closed, enjoy the moment and visualize all of your chakras from Muladhara to Sahasrara radiating their colours in perfect harmony. Feel them vibrating and radiating their light beyond your physical body, forming a healthy bright aura around you, like a protective shield of light. Stay here for a couple of breaths.

11. Now bring your attention to Sahasrara and, still keeping the big light around you, start reducing the colour violet to the size of a pea; then continue with Ajna, reducing the indigo-blue light to a size of a pea; continue doing this with all remaining chakras, and when you have finished with Muladhara, again visualize all of your chakras from bottom to top, and from top to bottom, like small colourful dots, with a radiant glowing aura around you.

12. Take a few more breaths here. Bring your palms together in front of your chest. Rub your hands together and place them on your eyes, then gently open your eyes and slowly bring your hands down. You are now ready to get on with your day.

Evening Ritual

While the morning chakra meditation prepares you for the day ahead, this evening chakra ritual prepares you physically, mentally and emotionally for bedtime and helps you to achieve a good night's sleep. A lot of people (me included) sometimes find it difficult to switch off completely from the day and let go of its experiences – that's actually quite normal. Lying in bed and thinking over an event that happened maybe ten or twelve hours earlier shows what emotional beings we are and how challenging it can be for us to detach from those emotions and experiences on a daily basis. Sometimes things that happened in the past still haunt us and steal our inner peace and sleep.

So this evening chakra meditation (and in principle any activity that we carry out before going to bed) should be about cleansing energetically, relaxing ourselves and nourishing our mind, body and soul. Throughout the day we pick up the energies of everyone and everything we have been in contact with, and some of those energies are absorbed by our chakras while others are left floating in our auric field, so we need to cleanse ourselves of them.

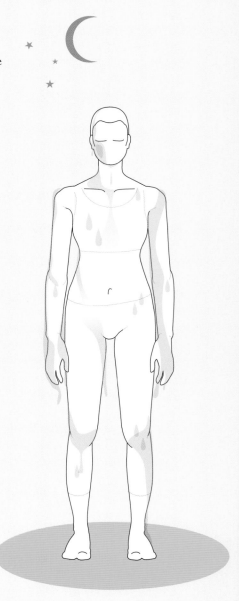

Duration: 15 minutes

1. Find a quiet, clean space. Stand firmly with your feet hip-width apart, or sit comfortably on a chair or on the floor. Make sure that your back is nice and straight. Relax your shoulders. Close your eyes. Bring awareness to your breath. Breathe normally – simply observe the quality of your breathing.

2. Bring awareness to your body, from your head to your toes, and from your toes to your head. Take this time as an opportunity to check in with yourself. Notice where in your body you are holding any tension. Is it in your forehead? Your jaw? Your shoulders? Your neck? Continue scanning your body, and use your breath to release those tensions from your body. Breathe into whichever area of your body needs attention, then breathe out. Release, let go... Stay here for as long as you need to, just breathing in and out deeply through your nose. Bring awareness to your entire being. Let go of the day and focus on being present in your mind, body and breath.

3. Visualize an influx of sparkly silver water showering you from above your head all the way down your body. While doing this, use your hands to gently brush off your body with top-down strokes (no up-and-down movements). Keeping your eyes closed and letting your body guide you, let your hands go where they need to. Visualize this cosmic water cleansing your mind of negative thoughts. Brush off your face, your throat, your chest, your arms, your abdomen, your lower abdomen, continuing all the way down the back and front of your body. Send those energies down to the Earth. Once you have finished, take a moment to notice how you feel after your "cosmic shower". How is your body feeling? And your mind? How are you feeling in your heart space?

4. Bring your palms together in front of your chest. Connect to the divine and say "Thank you" for your day, for the food on your plate, for the clothes you are wearing, for the roof over your head and for your good health. Take a moment to acknowledge your blessings. Be thankful for the day you had and the lessons you learned. Send love and light into your heart and let it expand within you. Send love and light to others and to the world. Be at peace within yourself, and with others. Smile. Everything will be okay.

There will be more about chakra healing later in the book (see pages 170–197) to provide you with the basic knowledge and tools that you need to perform chakra healing at home safely and with confidence.

"I am a natural healer. Within me lies the power to heal my mind, body and soul."

2

THE ENERGY BODY

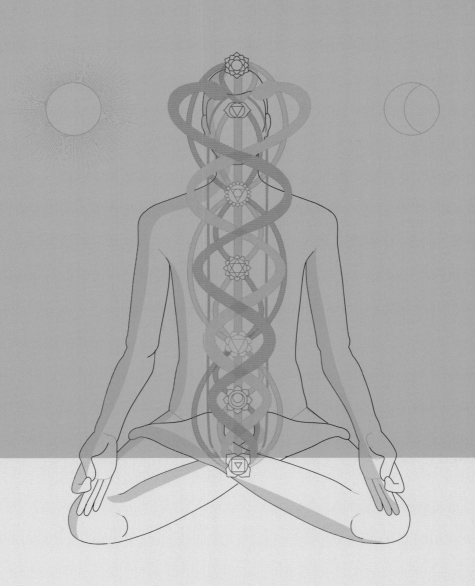

What Is the Energy Body?

The "energy body" consists of the invisible energies of the Spirit, mind and consciousness that affect and impact on all aspects of our life and wellbeing. The energy body is therefore an energy field around our physical body, made up essentially of the aura, the chakras and the subtle bodies. The aura is the electro-magnetic field around our body, which is nothing more than the emanation of energy from our chakras. The chakras are vortices of energy located in different parts of the body, and outside the physical body, including higher chakras such as the Earth Star Chakra (see page 168). In this book we are concentrating on the seven main chakras of the human body. The subtle bodies are layers of vibrating energy, each of which has its own vibration and purpose.

We are all very much aware of our physical body and are able to recognize and identify at least essential parts of our human anatomy, but what about the subtle body? What do we know about it? And how can we maintain a healthy energy body? Traditionally we have focused so much on our physical body that we have almost forgotten we are more than just a physical form of existence. There is a Spirit or soul within ourselves, and there is a powerful vital energy and life force that keeps our physical body alive and moving. We are energy bodies within a physical body that acts as a vehicle for the Spirit to experience the physical reality of existence.

The subtle body allows us to communicate with our physical body, to transmit information to other beings and receive information from them. Using this energy body we connect with the world around us and with the different levels of consciousness. From a holistic perspective, when there is not a good flow of energy, due to blockages or imbalances in our energy body, this will manifest in our physical body, causing all sorts of ailments and diseases, as well as fear, stress and anxiety.

All the physical and cosmic vibrations in the entire universe are echoed in our subtle etheric body. The subtle body further affects our physical body: we are designed to absorb and feed ourselves with these cosmic universal energies, but we must overcome our physical, mental, emotional and spiritual limitations – we must peel off the layers of the self. Working through the different levels of consciousness of existence, we open the channels to receive these high-vibrational energies.

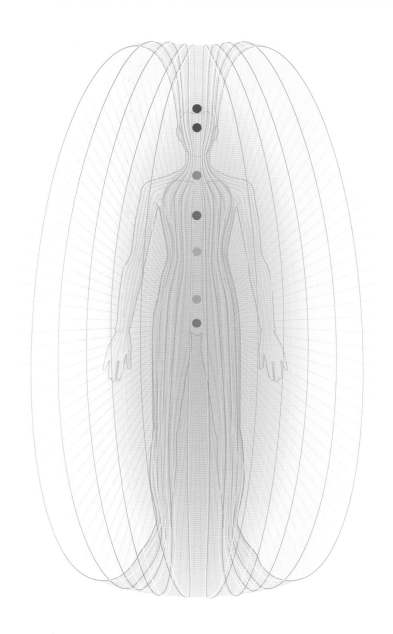

The Aura and the Seven Bodies

The aura is a bio-electric magnetic field that radiates from human beings, animals, plants and both living and non-living things. This electromagnetic field can extend for about an arm's length around the body. It extends above the head and below the feet into the ground. It has seven layers, and each layer is represented by a colour, density, shape, functionality and vibrational frequency. We call these seven layers the subtle or spiritual bodies of human beings, and they correspond to the seven dimensions of reality and to the chakra system. These layers have different density and vibrational frequencies. The further the auric body is from the physical body, the more subtle, light and high-frequency it is. These layers or subtle bodies are interrelated and affect one another, and so a state of imbalance in one of these bodies will directly affect the others.

The Aura

The aura is also called the "auric egg", due to its oval egg-shape. It is like a giant globe full of energy that emanates from the seven chakras in circles that intertwine. The more energy the aura emanates, the bigger the globe will be, and the more receptive it will be to the divine's consciousness. Your aura is like your spiritual skin. In the same way that your skin protects the organs and internal structures of your physical body, so when the aura is strong and radiant it shields you from the negative energy that surrounds you. Even the Earth has its own aura, which consists of all the thoughts and emotions of the people who inhabit it.

A person's aura can reveal their truest self, what they have done and even the great being they could become. We can understand the aura as the combined manifestation of the radiation of our chakras and the influence of the reflection of our Spirit. All these elements together create the magnetic field around the human body — that is to say, the human aura. The chakras radiate energy outside the physical body and their emanations are in the rainbow spectrum: the different colours of the chakras.

Aura colours can reveal information about your thoughts and feelings and come in different shades. Auras are not perceived by the physical eye — only by Ajna chakra or third eye. The aura can be seen by gifted people and those trained in the healing arts, although you can also see the aura by training your third eye to do so.

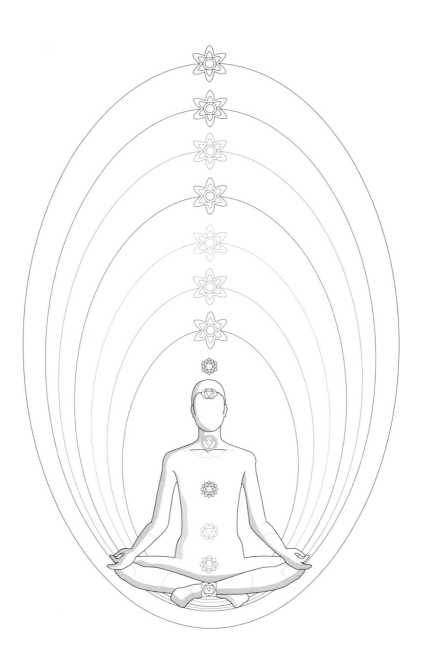

Aura Colours

Aura colours and meanings are based on the deepest colour and shade. The brighter and more radiant that colour is, the closer it is to representing the quality of a particular chakra, as it will be vibrating at the same frequency as the chakra. You may find that, apart from the seven colours of the chakras, there are also other hues and shades within the auric field, such as white, grey and pink. The colours in the aura represent the combination of energy emanating from the chakras and energies within the aura, so you may see a deep-red aura or a soft-red aura in someone, but the brighter they are, the healthier they are.

Do be aware that the meaning of the aura colours may vary in different texts, and this can be a bit confusing. For example, some people believe that a gold aura colour represents materialism – someone who is greedy and over-enjoying the pleasures in life – while others describe gold as a connection to the divine and to spirituality. The latter resonates with me more, so I use that explanation. Usually there is no right or wrong in spirituality; it is more a question of intuition and letting your inner wisdom guide you.

The Meaning of Aura Colours

- **Red aura**: This is associated with the physical body, sexuality, the heart and circulation. It is related to the physical world and is linked to Muladhara. It represents passion, power and connection.
- **Orange aura**: This is linked to the reproductive organs and to Svadhisthana. It represents creativity, stamina, lots of energy and excitement.
- **Yellow aura**: This is the colour of fire and energy-awakening. The associated chakra is Manipura. It is associated with intelligence, action and power and is also linked with the emotions, and on a physical level to the stomach and spleen.
- **Green aura**: This aura colour is related to the heart and lungs. It represents good health, growth and balance. It is linked to Anahata.
- **Blue aura**: This colour is related to Vishuddha and the thyroid gland. It is associated with clarity, communication and truth. An aura of this colour could suggest that that person is loving, caring and expressive.
- **Indigo-blue aura**: This relates to Ajna and is intuitive, visionary and sensitive. It is linked to the pineal gland, psychic abilities and spirituality, as well as the ability to see beyond the physical and spiritual world.

- **Violet aura**: This is related to Sahasrara, the pituitary gland and the nervous system. It is associated with an understanding of the self and a connection with the celestial beings and the Higher Self. It represents happiness, healing and sensitivity.
- **Pink aura**: This indicates a sensitive, sensual and loving energy. It represents affection and purity, friendship and compassion. It can be a representation of Anahata chakra.
- **Silver aura**: This is the colour of abundance in the physical and spiritual realms. It represents awakening to the cosmic universal energy.
- **Golden aura**: This is the colour of enlightenment and connection to the divine. It symbolizes wisdom, spirituality and divine guidance. People who are truly enlightened will have a silver or golden aura colour.
- **Black aura**: This usually indicates long-term pain, grief and suffering, plus a lack of forgiveness. It embodies dark entities, childhood trauma, past-life hurt and unreleased long-term issues. Negative auras such as black and grey can be fixed. We are here in this life to heal ourselves from past wounds, karma, negative emotions and anything that is not in alignment with the soul – so anything that is holding us back from evolving and expanding should be released. Having a very negative or dark aura is rare, although unfortunately there are people who are in a dark place in their lives, such as long-term criminals who don't show any remorse for their crimes or any intention of becoming a better individual; what they think is dark, what they say is dark and their actions are dark – their lives are literally stuck and there is no flow of energy. Unless there is a spontaneous or conscious spiritual awakening that makes the individual realize the path they are on, that person will remain in a negative emotional and mental state, so their energy will always be negative and dark.
- **White aura**: This is mostly seen in children and is another type of energy. It represents spirituality, purity and light, the higher dimensions and angelic qualities.
- **Grey aura**: This symbolizes stagnant energies and blockages.
- **Rainbow aura**: This is the colour of energy healers and starseed people, or highly evolved souls. Starseed people are believed to come from another dimension or planet. They are here to help us evolve.

How to See the Aura

My mother trained me to see the aura. I was in my mid-teens and I still remember listening to her saying, "Don't move. I can see your aura right now… It's a beautiful light blue." And I was saying in my head, "Yeah, right." She would spend hours looking at people's auras every time there was a family party or gathering at home. So while other kids were playing around in the neighbourhood, my sisters and I were taught to see people's auras. I kept it a secret at the time, otherwise my friends would call me *bruja* (a witch) or crazy. My sisters and I used to have such fun looking at each other's auras – my eldest sister was really good at it and picked it up quite quickly. I used to get frustrated that I couldn't see anything, but my mother would say, "Don't worry – you will see it when you are ready. You don't see the aura with your two eyes; you see it with your third eye chakra!" It took me some time until I finally saw my sister's green aura above her head and shoulders, and then again and again. I realized then that my mum wasn't crazy after all, and there was something mystical and supernatural about it that has captivated me ever since.

You can see the aura in two different ways:
- Through your Ajna chakra
- Through aura photography using a Kirlian camera

Seeing the Aura Through Your Ajna Chakra

This is an exercise that you can do regularly at home. Start by trying to see your own aura first, so that you know what are you looking for. Practise trying to see your hand's aura. Make sure you have a white wall or white background, then extend your arm in front of you and open your hand, with the palm facing you. Focus on one part of your hand, such as the little top square of your middle finger. Don't focus too hard; just let your gaze stay relaxed. You will start to see double and, unless it isn't comfortable, keep gazing softly at your focus point. You will begin to see a shadowy, subtle outline around the fingers. Keep gazing at the colour emerging, and not at the shadow. As you keep doing this, the colour will be intensifying.

Don't worry if you don't get it at first. As with most things in life, the more you practise it, the better you get at it. This exercise requires concentration and patience, and it might take you quite some time before you get it right. If you see a small outline, usually of the same colour, that's also okay. Give yourself time. There will be a point when you will be able to see different auras and their extensions. Or maybe you will be just like my mum, who is able to see people's auras without even looking for them.

To see someone's entire aura using the same method, ask the person to stand around 3m (10ft) away from you, then focus on their nose. Ask them to close their eyes so that you don't get distracted.

Aura Photography Using a Kirlian Camera

Aura photography is a spiritual service to enable people to see their auric or electromagnetic field; it captures the aura showing a beautiful array of colours. The Kirlian camera was invented by a Russian couple, Semyon and Valentina Kirlian, in 1939. At the time they were experimenting with electromagnetic fields of high intensity, when Semyon received an electric shock in one of his hands. When this accident happened, he noticed that there was an illuminated ring or halo around his hand that lasted for few seconds. This incident led the couple to further investigation and research around the world, and the Soviet Union sponsored the experiments. The first Kirlian cameras were duly manufactured and, after several trials, the couple came to the conclusion that the phenomenon was due to shooting at high voltage through an object that is connected to, or directly placed in contact with, the photographic film; the camera then registers the luminosity around the exposed object.

In 1970 Guy Coggins, an American entrepreneur, built an aura camera – the AuraCam 6000 – which adapted the Kirlians' methods to produce instant photographs. There are still around one hundred of these cameras in the world. Coggins's latest innovation is the home aura-detector WinAura. On social media such as Instagram you can find a good portfolio of aura photography.

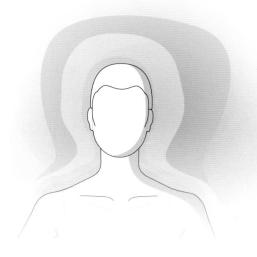

The Aura's Effects

Our aura is created by tiny energy currents that are associated with the etheric, mental and emotional body. These energy currents radiate from our body in all directions and have an influence over the physical body, causing it to react in a number of different ways. We can therefore understand that the aura is not just a halo around us, but also an extension of our being.

Our protective field consists of our own emanations, so we are the ones who determine its state. Your aura cannot lie – it shows the reality of your being in the present, either through its radiant light and colour or in the form of stains and shadows. This is why an Ascended Master knows with certainty which evolutionary level we are in, and what we really think, feel and do, just by looking at our aura. Ascended Masters are believed to be ascended beings who were once human and underwent a series of spiritual transformations here on Earth, leading to spiritual enlightenment.

There is a direct correlation between the quality of our thoughts, words, emotions and actions and the quality of our aura. The better we are as individuals, the more radiant and vast our energy will be and the brighter, bigger and healthier it will look. This aura will expand, affecting not only us, but also other beings, our surroundings and even the aura of the planet.

By using our thoughts, feelings, words and actions improperly or negatively, we create undesirable forms that can be retained in our aura, which can in turn poison our lives and the lives of people around us, our nation and our planet. For example, a person who is constantly complaining, being negative toward other people or situations, being materialistic and simply not acting with kindness throughout life will have an unhealthy aura, and this can manifest as dark marks, or a heavy and dense aura. On the other hand, if someone is always positive, kind, happy and has good thoughts toward other people and situations, this will reflect as a healthy aura, and it will be a light and radiant colour.

Sometimes you don't know why, but you feel comfortable being next to someone, even someone you have just met; or, on the contrary, you may feel uncomfortable around someone. This is because of their aura, or what we might normally call their "vibe". The aura constantly reflects our soul, our vibrational frequency and what we are made of energetically. It is the first thing we encounter when we see or meet someone. It is something that we are generally unaware of, as it happens in the quantum or spiritual realm and we can't simply put our minds into this.

Experiences of the Human Aura

We are constantly connecting and interacting with other people. Here are some of the signs of a universal human energy-field experience:

- You feel uncomfortable in large groups or crowds
- You feel uncomfortable around someone
- You feel anxious when you enter a room full of people
- You turn round and someone is staring at you
- You feel drained around certain people
- You feel at ease in someone's presence
- You feel irritable in someone's presence, without any particular reason

If you have had such emotions, then you have felt and experienced the auric field of another person or environment. We can also experience the energy field of animals, plants, crystals, and so on.

Today many people are the victims of other people's thoughts. The human being has an incredible potential to influence, and be influenced by, another's thoughts and aura. Through the aura, both evil and virtue can be observed; therefore we must protect our mind, our feelings and our actions in the same way that we protect ourselves physically. You can do this by reinforcing and sealing your aura.

It may be difficult to believe, but through the proper use of the mind and aura, a human being has the potential to manifest all their divine potential. If they succeed in establishing an internal communication with others' three superior bodies (the etheric, astral and mental body), this will add to their aura beautiful radiant colours that potentiate the radiation of their aura and will give them the capacity to heal anyone who comes in contact with it.

The Seven Bodies

Each subtle body connects into the physical body through an energy centre or chakra via the *nadis*, which are our energy channels. The seven subtle bodies work like the vehicles of your soul. They are:

- Physical body
- Etheric body
- Astral body
- Mental body
- Spiritual body
- Cosmic body
- Nirvanic body

There are other bodies beyond this level, which are the celestial bodies, but they lie beyond our comprehension at this level of evolution and consciousness. It is believed that the seven bodies of mankind are developed within a period of 49 years. During the first 25 years of life we are supposed to develop the first four bodies; and in the next 24 years we are supposed to search for the other three bodies. This is our quest in life: to evolve and ascend from the Lower Self to the Higher Self and beyond.

The Physical Body

The physical body is known as well as the "food body" in yogic traditions. It is the body that we can see and touch. With this body we can feel the physical experiences in our lives and interact with others physically. Muladhara is associated with this body and represents primal instincts, survival, feeling safe and basic needs; this first chakra represents the foundation of our being. Our physical body forms the foundation for us to live in the physical world and develops in the first seven years of life when the other bodies are dormant, becoming awakened only later in life. The first seven years of a human being are quite limited, and it is during these years that we learn the necessary tools for survival, such as talking, walking, feeding ourselves, controlling our toilet needs, and so on.

The Etheric Body

The etheric body is also known as the "emotional body" and is connected to the second chakra, Svadhisthana. This body develops in years 7–14. These seven years represent the emotional growth of an individual. Puberty and sexual maturity are reached during this time. Strong emotions such as fear, hate, anger and violence develop. All these are qualities of the second body and are necessary for survival. Fear, violence and anger are necessary in the emotional realm, otherwise one could not survive. If someone stagnates at the second body, then the opposite emotions, such as love, forgiveness and fearlessness, don't develop.

The Astral Body

The astral body is linked to our third chakra, Manipura. It is formed between the ages of 14 and 21. During this period our reasoning, intellect and thinking are developed. We could say that after the development of the second body someone reaches adulthood, although this adulthood isn't complete until the third body is formed. At this stage people are pretty much responsible for their own actions. During these seven years a person will make choices that might impact upon them later in life: they are allowed to drive, to vote, to drink, and so on. Twenty-one years are required for the development of the astral body, but the majority of people don't develop any further. Manipura is the last chakra of matter, and most people don't go beyond the physical and material planes; their growth stops on this plane, and there is no further development for the rest of their lives. The physical, etheric and astral bodies are also associated with the Lower Self.

The Mental Body

The mental body, or the psyche, is the fourth subtle body and is connected to our fourth chakra, Anahata. It develops between the ages of 21 and 28. This is the body made of thoughts and all things intellectual: how we use words and how we process information. Some of the qualities of the fourth body include clarity, connection and the ability to see through illusions. This is the body connected to imagination, dreaming and vision. Imagination and dreaming happen in the mind, but a very well-developed imagination can lead to vision, and vision to action. This body is the key element in thoughts becoming reality in our lives, and is therefore key in the society we live in. If our thoughts are connected to our heart — that is, if our thoughts are coming from a place of love and integrity — so are our intentions and actions.

The Spiritual Body

The fifth body is the spiritual body, which is related to Vishuddha. This subtle body represents our connection to all things, including the self, the Earth, the universe and beyond. It connects us to all that is. This body provides spiritual guidance and connection to the Higher Self and spiritual realm. Duality ends with the fifth body, which doesn't have two possibilities, but only one. As long as there is proper growth in life, by the age of 35 this body may be fully developed, although most people remain in the third body, or third layer of consciousness. If we are unaware of the fourth body, or Anahata, then the spiritual body remains dormant and unknown; we must overcome the challenges of the physical world to be able to arrive in Anahata, which cleanses and purifies the mind, because those thoughts will eventually become words and actions. A fully developed spiritual body acknowledges that there is a higher force guiding us, and has the ability to see and understand that there is only one truth to connect with. The limitations of the first four bodies are transcended and the soul becomes free.

The Cosmic Body

The cosmic body is the sixth subtle body of man. It is linked to Ajna or the third eye chakra. This body holds the essence of the soul or Spirit – the part of you that is of God. The natural development of this body can occur at the age of 42. The person evolves beyond the self. There's is total liberation of the Atman, or self. The seven bodies prove that ultimately we are in a continual quest of self-realization to achieve Nirvana, or freedom from suffering. To understand the layers of the subtle bodies you must realize that the only purpose for us being here is to go back to the Source: that highest consciousness where we come from, and unity with God and beyond. To achieve this, we must overcome the challenges and limitations of the physical, etheric, astral and mental bodies. We must transcend the seven bodies – or at least that's the goal of the self.

The first quest of the seeker is to get rid of the pain, hatred, violence and suffering from the levels up to the fifth body. Once this is achieved, the search continues to get rid of the self on the next three remaining bodies.

The Nirvanic Body

The word Nirvana means the "end of the flame" or "end of the blaze". This body represents nothingness and non-existence. It is connected to Sahasrara. This body goes beyond existence and self; on this body there is no self and no God. This layer is so subtle and thin that it almost doesn't exist – everything disappears here. The fifth body is the gateway of liberation leading to the sixth body, a state of God realization, and then the quest for liberation of the soul disappears. This body goes beyond the cosmos back to the original source, or whatever came before creation.

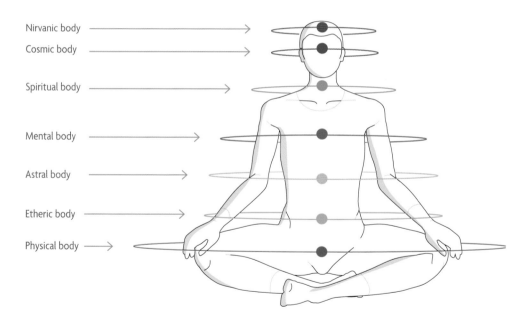

Nirvanic body

Cosmic body

Spiritual body

Mental body

Astral body

Etheric body

Physical body

How to Protect Your Aura

In order to have a healthy, glowing aura, we must be aware of it, acknowledge that it is there and that it protects us energetically. We need to protect our aura from our own thoughts and actions, as well as from the thoughts and actions of others. Cleansing and protecting your energy field regularly is a good practice. Think about your aura as the little home where you live, and in the same way that you lock your home when you go out, to protect it from robbery and have a peace of mind while you are out, you should lock and protect your aura to keep everything inside it safe – and this includes your soul, your physical, emotional and mental body, your organs and glands, and so on. If you care about your physical belongings, why wouldn't you care about your spiritual wellbeing too? We are spiritual beings living a physical experience, and your physical reality is the manifestation of what is going on inside you. Everything starts within.

There are five powerful ways to cleanse and protect your aura from negativity: prayer, visualization, an aura-cleansing bath or shower, aura-combing and smudging. There are other ways to cleanse and protect your aura, such as by having a sun bath or a walk in the rain, and by chanting mantras. However, these five methods are the most popular ones and are easy to do at home, with no need to go outside.

Prayer

Prayers are very powerful when they are said with intention and conviction. And connecting regularly with your angel or spirit guide and praying for it to step forward and be by your side throughout the day is a powerful protection. Prayers are very personal because they come from the deepest part of you. Instead of me giving you a list of prayers, I invite you to research some prayers and choose the one that resonates best with you: read some texts, search online or try to create your own prayer. When I was a little girl I had an angel revelation in a dream, and when I told my mother, she said that my dream was a verse of the Bible. It was in fact a verse from the apocalyptic chapter, and the angel I saw was St Michael Archangel. My mum gave me an angel figurine and taught me a prayer. Forty years on, I still recite the same St Michael Archangel prayer every time I leave home or walk into a challenging situation where I feel I need spiritual guidance and protection. I firmly believe in it and am convinced that I have been saved from harm and danger by my angel twice in my life, after calling on St Michael.

Visualization

Before leaving home, before facing a challenging day or meeting or before entering a negative place, protect yourself energetically and raise your vibration. This is a powerful visualization meditation.

1. Find a quiet space. Take a moment to connect with your entire being, close your eyes, then inhale deeply through your nose and exhale deeply through your mouth. Visualize your energy field all around you. Imagine a white light above your head about an arm's length away, pulsing and contracting; as you breathe in and out, imaging the beam of light swirling and expanding as it slowly starts descending your body, leaving wide white rings around it (like sticky tape wrapping all round your body).

2. Let the white light go all the way down to below your feet, then up and down again, sealing you in. There is not part of you that is not protected by this divine white light. Visualize yourself inside a gigantic white egg of pure bright light, feeling held, safe and protected. Take a deep inhalation through your nose, and then exhale through your nose. Now say this out loud, "I am now surrounded by divine light. I trust my angels, spirit guides and Ascended Masters are supporting me today on every step."

Aura-cleansing Bath or Shower

Our auras exchange and pick up different types of energies (emotions) from people and situations around us. It is normal and very common for the aura to get stressed and cluttered with all of these. If the aura isn't cleaned, you might start feeling anxious, tired, irritated and negative. Luckily we can clear all these emotions from our electromagnetic field. I love an aura-cleansing bath. Here is the method:

1. Fill the bath with hot water (as hot as you can tolerate), adding a few drops of eucalyptus or lavender essential oil. Add a cup of Epsom salts or Himalayan sea salt, plus a cup of bicarbonate of soda.

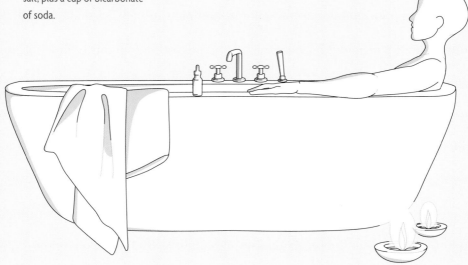

2. Soak yourself in the bath for up to 20 minutes maximum (people taking magnesium supplements should consult their doctor first). Alternatively, you can take a shower and imagine the water healing and cleansing your entire aura.

3. Imagine all the dirt and dark water going down the drain. Say aloud, "I'm cleansing my aura with this fresh water and releasing all the unwanted energies right now." You can end with a quick cold shower. You should feel like new!

Aura-combing

I learned this method from my mother when I was young. As a spiritual healer, she would aura-comb throughout the day in between clients. You can also use a selenite wand (a white crystal in a stick shape, for cleansing the aura) instead of your hands to stroke or comb your aura, following the same method as below.

1. Wash your hands. Find a quiet space. Stand firmly on your feet (if you are unable to stand up, sit on a chair with both feet on the ground and your back straight). Apply a few drops of essential oil such as frankincense, sandalwood or sage to the palm of your hands, them rub them together.

2. Visualize your aura. Start stroking, or combing, in one direction from the top of your head, hovering over your body, your arms, between your legs, over the back and front of your body. Tap the unwanted energy onto the ground. Keep doing this for a couple of minutes, visualizing your aura getting cleansed.

3. Say out loud, "I am releasing negative energies. I am releasing the energies that don't belong to me, I am releasing energies that don't serve me good. I am cleansing and purifying my aura. I am a being of love and light."

Smudging

This is a very ancient practice. The smoke of burning herbs and sacred wood is believed to have purifying, cleansing and protective benefits. If you have a well-ventilated space or the size of your room enables you to do this, then it is something you will enjoy. The strong smell of the herbs or sacred wood burning has physical, mental and spiritual benefits. Use a similar method to aura-combing (see opposite), doing the strokes over your body with the herbs or sacred wood instead.

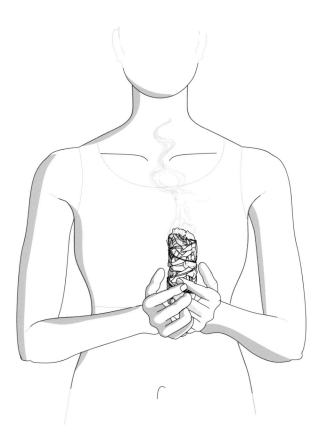

"My aura radiates love and light. It is in perfect harmony with my Higher Self and the universe."

The *Nadis*

The *nadis* in the yogic tradition (or the meridians in Chinese medicine) are not nerves, but rather pathways or channels for the flow of conscious energy. The literal meaning of *nadi* is "flow", and just as the negative and positive forces of electricity flow through complex circuits, so our *prana* flows freely through the *nadis*. *Nadis* are found in the astral body (see page 48), made up of astral subtle matter that carries the psychic currents. Since the *nadis* are not composed of any physical matter and are not ordinary physical nerves, they can't be seen in the physical body.

Prana shakti (vital force) and *manas shakti* (mental force) flow through every part of our body, from its complex organs to the smallest units, via the *nadis*. According to the Tantras, there are more than 72,000 *nadis* in the human body. They form a very complex energy network, where the energy flows like an electric current from one point to another. These 72,000 *nadis* cover the whole body, and through them the inherent rhythms of activity in the different organs are maintained.

Within this labyrinth of *nadis* there are 14 main channels; and of these, three are the most important for the control of energy flow to all other *nadis* in the body. These *nadis* are:

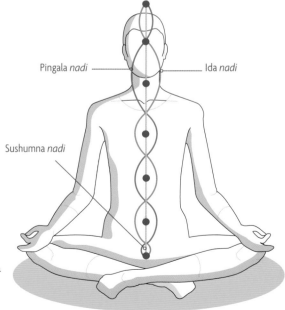

Pingala *nadi*

Ida *nadi*

Sushumna *nadi*

- **Ida nadi**: Located on the left side of the body, this is a cool energy associated with the Moon, night, the parasympathetic nervous system and feminine energy (known as *shakti*).
- **Pingala nadi**: Located on the right side of the body, this is a hot energy associated with the Sun, day, the sympathetic nervous system and masculine energy (known as Shiva).
- **Sushumna nadi**: Located in the middle of the body, this *nadi* originates from Muladhara and ends at the top of the head at Sahasrara. This is what we know as our central nervous system.

Ida nadi flows from the left side of Muladhara in spirals, passing through each chakra and forming a criss-cross pathway that terminates at the left side of Ajna. Pingala nadi flows from the right side of Muladhara, mirroring Ida and terminating at the right side of Ajna. These criss-crosses or intersections formed by the Ida and Pingala nadis along Sushumna nadi create the energy centres or chakras.

Yoga practices such as Hatha, Kundalini and Nadi Shodhana pranayama (alternate-nostril breathing, see page 272) focus on bringing balance between these two nadis, Ida and Pingala, and ultimately bring balance to the body and the central nervous system. When we balance Ida and Pingala, we are activating Sushumna nadi, which in turn activates the brain and spine. This total balance in the body brings a sense of complete happiness and health into our being. Sushumna nadi is the most important of all the nadis. It is also known as Brahma (God) nadi. It is analogous to the central spinal cord. The awakened Kundalini (see page 62) should rise up through the Sushumna nadi if it is already purified, and not through Ida or Pingala nadi.

It is estimated that most human beings use just 10 per cent of the brain's capacity. Imagine if we could access the full 100 per cent? The brain has ten compartments, nine of which are dormant, plus one that is active. The nine-tenths, situated at the front of the brain, are known as the inactive or sleeping brain. The reason for this is a lack of energy in this area. Both Ida and Pingala nadis supply energy to the active portion of the brain, whereas the other nine-tenths have only Pingala (masculine) energy. Pingala is life and Ida is consciousness. In order to awaken those nine dormant compartments we must charge the frontal part of the brain with sufficient prana by balancing Ida and Pingala and thus activating Sushumna nadi.

Practising pranayama, or breath control, regularly and consistently for a long period of time can arouse the silent areas. Regular practice of Kundalini yoga is also key in awakening the chakras and Sushumna nadi. In the same way that you have to flick a switch to turn on a lamp, so you have to flick the switches located in the chakras to awaken the sleeping brain.

A genius is one who has been able to awaken one or more of the dormant areas. When the whole brain wakes up, you become a total genius or junior god.

The *Pancha Koshas*

As we are now learning more about the subtle body, I would like to cover briefly the subject of the five bodies, because according to yogic tradition we are made up of these five bodies, and together they form an entire material and consciousness existence. The human body comprises two eternal forces: consciousness and matter. In yoga tradition, the consciousness of existence is called Purusha and is represented as a masculine force, and Prakriti is the feminine force that represents matter and nature. Both consciousness and matter are essential in the world; they are also known as Shiva and Shakti, the divine eternal father and the divine mother. Purusha never changes, whereas Prakriti is changeable. They are the two faces of one reality. The aim of yoga is to achieve Purusha – the eternal that represents the detachment from matter.

Pancha koshas (*pancha* means five and *kosha* = layer/sheath) are the five bodies, or five dimensions, of existence that seemingly cover the Atman (the self of consciousness): "the layers of the self". Each *kosha* vibrates at a different speed, and they interact and overlap with each other:

- **Physical layer/Annamaya** *kosha*: This is the physical body, composed of food and organic components: the body that we see, touch and feel.
- **Energy layer/Pranamaya** *kosha*: This is the body made of *prana*/energy or vital force.
- **Mental layer/Manomaya** *kosha*: This is the layer that comprises the mind and five sensory organs.
- **Wisdom layer/Vijnanamaya** *kosha*: This is the body that is made of intellect. This layer represents the combination of intellect and the five sense organs.
- **Bliss layer/Anandamaya** *kosha*: This is the body that comprises supreme bliss. It is the subtlest of the five *koshas* and is a reflection of the soul.

The ultimate goal of yoga is to achieve Purusha (beyond the five bodies, beyond duality and beyond consciousness), so we start from the outer body on our way to the fifth layer. Yoga traditions provide different tools and techniques to bring the five bodies into harmony, to nurture and detox us, so that we can reach the fifth body and, ultimately, God.

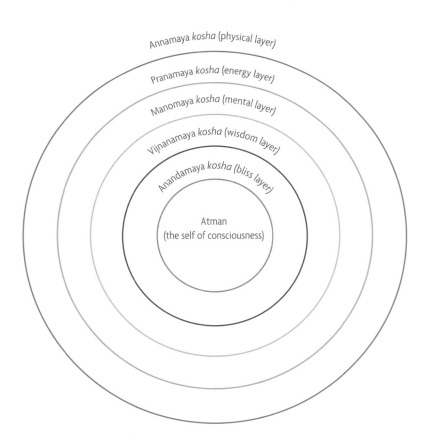

Annamaya *kosha* (physical layer)

Pranamaya *kosha* (energy layer)

Manomaya *kosha* (mental layer)

Vijnanamaya *kosha* (wisdom layer)

Anandamaya *kosha* (bliss layer)

Atman
(the self of consciousness)

Kundalini Energy

Kundalini is the dormant potential force in the human body that is situated at the root of the spinal column. In the masculine body it is in the perineum, and in the female body it is located at the root of the uterus, in the cervix. This area is known as the Muladhara chakra.

In Sanskrit, Kundalini means "coiled snake", so Kundalini is mostly referred to as a dormant snake at the base of our body, but is also often called the "sleeping goddess". In Hinduism, Kundalini is a form of divine feminine energy – a force or power associated with the divine feminine. This energy, when cultivated and awakened through Tantric practice, is believed to lead to spiritual liberation. The serpent power does not belong to the physical body or the mental body; it is in fact in the causal body (one of the three layers of the soul: physical, astral and causal). The causal body is the most subtle of the three and is contained within the other two: it lies beyond the concept of matter, time and space.

When Kundalini awakens, whether consciously or by accident, it rises from the lower chakra and travels up the spinal column (Sushumna nadi), piercing each of the chakras and giving each one an energetic boost. The rising of Kundalini starts from Muladhara and ends in Sahasrara. With the awakening of Kundalini there is a dawning of creative intelligence and an awakening of supramental faculties. By activating Kundalini you may become anything in life.

This potential force, which is a small part of divine cosmic Kundalini energy, enters the embryo along with the soul soon after conception. After completing the assigned task of creating the body of the baby in the womb, it lies dormant in the coiled shape in Muladhara. When we awaken this potential energy we are able to work toward the light of knowledge and enlightenment.

Kundalini is known as the most dangerous type of yoga because Kundalini yoga deals with this powerful cosmic energy and, once it's awakened, you open yourself up to a real and ultimate spiritual experience. When Kundalini rises up through the chakras you are opening the channels to bring light from the cosmos down through the crown and into the chakras, and you open up to higher guidance to allow freshness and insight to come in. A vision of God may take place, and the awakening of superpower faculties. To activate Kundalini you must prepare physically, emotionally, mentally and spiritually to be able to support and hold this energy within your body.

Kundalini awakening can happened either consciously or spontaneously. There are many people who have awoken their Kundalini, but most people are not completely prepared for this experience. The awakening of Kundalini represents the communion between Shiva and Shakti – two great forces within you – and the understanding of truth behind the appearance.

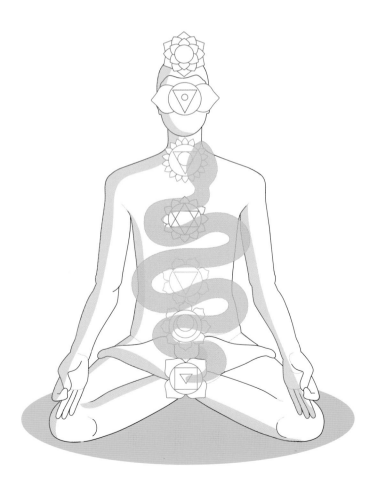

Awakening the Kundalini

There are different methods to awaken Kundalini, and they include the following:

- Birth
- Mantras
- Tapasya (austerity)
- Herbs
- Raya yoga (also known as Ashtanga yoga, the path of self-discipline and practice)
- *Pranayama* (breath control)
- *Kriya* yoga (*kriya* means "action", therefore *kriya* yoga is the yoga of action that rapidly accelerates spirituality in the aspirant)
- Tantric initiation
- Shaktipat (spiritual consciousness initiation)
- Self-surrender

Awakening Kundalini isn't that easy. It requires a lot of self-preparation and self-discipline. *Kriya* yoga is considered to be the most powerful and risk-free method that is suitable for modern-day humans. The purpose of *kriya* yoga is to awaken the chakras, purify the *nadis* and, finally, awaken the Kundalini *shakti*. *Shakti* is a powerful energy that an average person would find difficult to handle.

To awaken the Kundalini you must prepare yourself through yogic techniques such as *asanas*, *pranayama*, *kriyas* and meditation. All of these can offer you a smooth and relatively risk-free Kundalini awakening. Regular practice of these Tantric techniques will help you expand your awareness and awakening of dormant areas of the brain, so that you can understand what is happening to you and how to handle the Kundalini *shakti* rising up the Sushumna *nadi* and activating the chakras.

I haven't personally experienced a complete Kundalini arising yet, although I have experienced a partial activation of the Sushumna *nadi* and a mild Kundalini awakening. The best way to explain my experience is to describe it as a current of heat rising slowly from the base of my spine. This was during a powerful Kundalini practice involving mantras, *pranayama*, *kriyas*, *mudras* and *asanas* that we were executing on my four-week Kundalini teacher-training course in Rishikesh in northern India. I remember feeling an unusual metallic taste/smell in my mouth and nose first, and this was followed by an intense heat developing at my tailbone and moving up through my spine. The heat stopped at Manipura and I felt an incredible feeling of inner peace and happiness. I felt content and surrendered to the divine power of *shakti* energy. I knew in a way what I was experiencing, because of my regular *sadhana* (sadhana means spiritual practice that is done daily to attain knowledge or a goal – usually spiritual development and detachment from worldly things), and I am now confident that my entire being can hold this energy in a much better way and, most importantly, in a safe way.

You should use regular purification and detoxifying of the body, meditation, *pranayama* and specific *kriyas* and *asanas* for this purpose. All these practices should be done regularly and consistently, and for long period of time, before attempting a Kundalini awakening.

The first step in awakening the Kundalini is cleansing the chakras and dissolving any energy blockages within them, in order to awaken the chakras. When the chakras are awakened, the experience is very pleasant and comfortable. The Ida and Pingala *nadis* must also be balanced regularly. This can be achieved by regular *pranayama*, such as Nadi Shodhana breathing (see page 272). All these practices, when done safely and regularly, are preparing your body and mind for the next higher practice.

Within Kundalini yoga, the ancient and Tantric techniques of breath exercises, visualizations, *mudras*, *bandhas* (body locks), *kriyas*, *asanas* and mantras are focused on manipulating the flow of energy through the chakras.

Rules and Preparation for Kundalini Awakening

- Vegetarian diet
- Early-morning *sadhana*
- A clean and peaceful place to practise in
- *Asanas* for Kundalini
- Discipline: practise daily at the same time
- Chakra *sadhana* (daily/regular practice of the stimulation, awakening and purification of the chakras, usually practised in a systematic order, continuously and for a long period of time)

3

THE

CHAKRAS

Aspects of the Chakras

The chakras, our energy centres, are vortices of *prana* within our bodies and outside them, controlling and regulating the flow of energy in the human structure. We are focusing here principally on the seven main chakras because these are the ones that directly affect our physical, mental and emotional body; and, according to their location in the human body, they relate to certain organs and glands, as well as to systems in our bodies. Chakras are also linked to specific areas of the brain, and are connected to the incredible network of psychic channels called *nadis*.

The chakras are represented by lotus flowers, each having a particular number of petals that are inscribed with *bija* mantras. There are six important aspects of each chakra:

- The colour
- The petals of the lotus flower
- The *yantra* (a geometrical shape used for meditation and to achieve higher levels of consciousness)
- The *bija* mantra (*bija* means "seed", and a *bija* mantra is a one-syllable sound that, when chanted aloud, can activate and purify the chakras)
- The animal symbol
- The higher or divine symbol

The Five Elements

Something very important you should know about the chakras is that they are linked to, or associated with, the different elements of the universe. According to yogic philosophy, the "five elements" are the basis of our creation. We are made of the five elements, and through our yoga practice we can bring balance between these elements within our bodies.

All yogic practices derive from the fundamentals of Bhuta Shuddhi – or cleansing the elements so slowly that you come to a state of mastery over the five elements. These elements together constitute the universe, and as we are part of that universe or a manifestation of it, we are also made of the five elements. Everything around us is a form of manifestation of these five elements. Imbalances of the elements in our bodies can impact negatively on both our physical body and our emotional body. Regular practice of yoga, breathing exercises and mudras can help to maintain the balance and harmony in our bodies. The qualities of each chakra are influenced by the elements. The bija mantras are the sound not of the chakras themselves, but of the elements in each chakra.

In the human body 72 per cent of us is water, and it is in sync with the planet. Approximately 72 per cent of the planet comprises water, too. And this is how life has evolved. Of the remaining components, 12 per cent of our body is Earth, 6 per cent is air, another 4 per cent is fire and the remaining 6 per cent is space.

A good practice to start bringing awareness to the five elements in our bodies, and cleansing them, is to observe how you consume these elements. How do you treat them? The whole system of ancient cultures was about treating the four traditional elements – Earth, Fire, Water and Air – correctly.

Earth Element

The Earth element is the one most closely linked to our physical world, and is the densest of all the elements. It governs money, property, business, security, loyalty, responsibility and everything that relates to the physical body and wellbeing. This is the feminine element of Mother Earth and represents stability and growth; it forms the basis on which the other elements move.

The Earth is a receptive energy, which helps us to accept our responsibilities and call our attention to the limitations of our inner power. The season of the Earth is winter and its compass direction is the north. In the natural environment the place of Earth is a cave, a symbol of refuge, the womb, rebirth and home to the ancient oracles. Other places associated with this element are the forests, valleys and fields. It is the element associated with financial institutions, gatherings and business. The energies of the Earth element are rooted, and people of this element love to be surrounded by family and are quite tactile. But an overabundance of this element slows things down and progress is limited. Too little of it causes an inability to dare, take risks or diversify.

Other attributes of the Earth element include the following:
- Associated with Muladhara, so a blocked root chakra is represented by a lack of this Earth energy in our bodies.
- Bija mantra = LAM.
- Represented in our bodies by toxins, bones and solid muscle.
- The Earth element in our hands is represented by the ring finger. Mudras using this finger can balance this element in our bodies.
- The zodiac signs associated with the Earth element are Taurus, Virgo and Capricorn.
- Music and sounds that tap into the energy of this element are tribal music, drums, strong beats, nature and birds. In general, rainforest sounds can stimulate this element.
- The colour that represents the Earth element is green.

Tapping into the energy of the Earth element is about spending time in nature and connecting with it and bringing a bit of nature into your home. Having a plant in your house, apartment or over the desk can make significant improvements if you are off-balance in this element.

Water Element

The element of Water affects the subconscious, the emotions and dreams. It's also the element of love. Constantly active below the surface, it influences our moods and emotional responses. The element of Water governs the west and its season is autumn; it purifies, heals, cleanses, offers emotional release and eliminates everything that is stagnant. The energy of Water is feminine, is symbolized by the womb and is related to fertility. In a household, the bathroom and sink in the kitchen are governed by this element; it also relates to the living room and to areas of social activity, like an art gallery.

Water is the element of healing environments. Its places are the sea, lakes, rivers, ponds and areas where the earth is soaked with rain. Water personalities are spiritual, emotional, sensitive and highly intuitive. They approach life from a perspective of their feelings, and can be quite spontaneous. A lack of the Water element in our bodies can make us emotionally remote, with an inability to express ourselves, which keeps people at a distance. In this case they would be less empathetic, intuitive and psychic. Too much Water, on the other hand, carries all emotions to the extreme, making daily functioning in the world difficult, and possibly causing psychic overload.

Other attributes of the Water element include the following:
- Associated with Svadhisthana, the sacral chakra.
- *Bija* mantra = VAM.
- Represented by all the fluids and water present in our bodies.
- The Water element in our hands is represented by the little finger. *Mudras* using this finger can balance this element in our bodies.
- The zodiac signs associated with water element are Cancer, Scorpio and Pisces.
- Music and sounds that tap into the energy of this element are waterfall, ocean and rain sounds. Water drops, trumpets, pipes and electric guitars can stimulate this element.
- The colour that represents the Water element is blue.

Tapping into the energy of the Water element is about spending time by the sea, lakes or rivers, taking nourishing baths and bringing a bit of the Water element into your life by making sure you keep yourself well hydrated.

Fire Element

The element of Fire is associated with the Sun, the giver of life; it governs passions, intensity, desire, intuition, understanding, possibilities, action and inner power. The Fire element cleanses and purifies, can create or destroy, and may consume everything in its way. It's the only one of the elements that cannot exist without feeding on something else. It offers heat and cooking, but can get out of control, and has the power to transform everything it touches.

The Fire element dominates the south and is related to motivation, creativity and passion. It has a fast and powerful energy. It's positive and uplifting, but it can be scary if it gets out of control. It is the creative spark within all of us and promotes courage and strength, helping us fight for what we want. Fire personalities are charming, charismatic and passionate; they live life to the maximum and depend to a large extent on their instincts and intuitions. Fire strengths are creativity and leadership; bold in their career and love life, Fire personalities like stimulation and challenge in both areas. However, too much Fire can be destructive because no limits are imposed, leaving the Fire entity worn and unbalanced. An overabundance of Fire leads to selfishness, egocentricity and unrealistic expectations of others. Too little Fire leads to low energy and a lack of motivation and initiative.

Other attributes of the Fire element include the following:
- Associated with Manipura, the solar plexus chakra.
- *Bija* mantra = RAM.
- Represented in our bodies by the heat generated in the digestive system.
- The Fire element in our hands is represented by the thumb. *Mudras* using this finger can balance this element in our bodies.
- The zodiac signs associated with the Fire element are Aries, Leo and Sagittarius.
- Music and sounds that tap into the energy of this element are the cello, violin, guitar. Sounds of an open fire can stimulate this element in our bodies.
- The colour that represents the Fire element is red.

Tapping into the energy of the Fire element is about spending time by an open fire, contemplating and appreciating that moment, enjoying the sun's rays, carefully sunbathing, observe the sunrise, lighting a candle. All these activities can help you connect with this element.

Air Element

The Air element rules the kingdom of the mind and all mental activity, and is the most ethereal element. Its direction is the east, and its seasonal station is spring. As it is the element of the wind, Air governs all movement and is associated with travel, freedom, thought, ideas, intellect, imagination and discovery. The areas governed by the Air element are meeting rooms, schools, libraries, airports and train stations. It's related to mathematics, science and law. Places of the Air element are the summits of mountains, windy plains, clear and cloudy skies.

People of this element are rational and analytical; they are clear thinkers and enjoy mental stimulation, a good debate and an exchange of ideas. Too much air, however, creates a critical perspective and a pedantic attitude toward all things, plus a lack of sympathy toward others and a judgemental attitude. These personalities can muffle ideas in the early stages, without any kind of rationality. An overabundance of the element of Air can lead someone to live in a fantasy world, given to ideas that have no substance. They can get close to something that is unsustainable and are blind to its pitfalls.

Other attributes of the Air element include the following:
- Associated with Anahata, the heart chakra.
- *Bija* mantra = YAM.
- Represented in our bodies by the oxygen and gases that are exchanged there.
- The Air element in our hands is represented by the index finger. *Mudras* using this finger can balance this element in our bodies.
- The zodiac signs associated with this element are Gemini, Libra and Aquarius.
- Music and sounds that tap into the energy of this element are the sounds of the wind and string instruments sounds such as the harp, violin and piano. These sounds can stimulate and raise the energy levels of this element in our bodies.
- The colours that represent the Air element are white or light blue.

At home you can tap into the energy of the Air element by opening the windows and letting fresh air into your home. Activities that stimulate your mind and intellect, such as crosswords and puzzles, reading a book and analytical games will also help you connect with this element.

Ether or Spiritual Element

The fifth element is the Spirit. In Sanskrit this is Akasha, and that's where the term "Akashic Records" comes from: a record of knowledge belonging to the material plane, which exists in the astral realm. In the Middle Ages Ether was referred to as the fifth element. The quest of alchemists was to find this element, which they believed contained the secret of eternal life. Ether is described as the substance that formed the heavens. The qualities of the Spirit are expressed through art, music, writing, religion, healing and magic. Spirit is the element that is most difficult to describe, because it is everywhere and nowhere. It is the force that unites all things. The Spirit allows us to go beyond our self-limitations and open our minds.

Other attributes of the Spirit element include the following:
- Associated with the Ajna and Sahasrara chakras.
- *Bija* mantra = OM/AUM.
- Represented in our bodies by the space in our cells.
- The Ether element in our hands is represented by the middle finger. *Mudras* using this finger might balance this element in our bodies.
- There are no zodiac signs related to this element. However, Ether is the union of all elements so we could think of this element as the space holder for all elements and zodiac signs.
- Music and sounds that can stimulate and balance this element in our bodies are wind instruments like the flute and whistle. Bells and chimes can also help to connect with this element.

At home you can embody this element by doing activities that represent union and unification to you. These could be activities with your family, the community or other meaningful connections.

"I bring balance into my entire being by tapping into the energy of the five elements. I am Earth, Water, Fire, Air and Spirit. These elements are in perfect harmony within me."

First Chakra: Muladhara or Root Chakra

MULADHARA ASSOCIATIONS

Name: *Mul* = root, origin, essence; *Adhara* = place

Qualities: Survival, courage, stability, basic needs, safety, sexuality, family love, instinct

Location: At the perineum in the male body, and at the cervix in the female body; the pelvic plexus

Organs/systems: Secretory organs, genitals, bladder, colon/large intestine, kidneys, arterial blood, left chamber of the heart; skeletal system, circulatory system, muscular system

Endocrine glands: Adrenal cortex/adrenal glands

Colour: Red/crimson

Flower: Four petals

Element: Earth

Deities: Brahma, Dakini, Ganesha

Mantra: LAM

Sense: Smell

Sensory organ: Nose

Organ of activity: Anus

Animal: Elephant

Food: Red apples, cherries, strawberries, red onions, raspberries, tomatoes, pomegranates, watermelons, beetroots, red grapes, red peppers, radishes, red potatoes

Musical note: C

Crystals: Garnet, red jasper, black tourmaline, black obsidian, smoky quartz, haematite, bloodstone

Essential oils: Sandalwood, black pepper, cedar, clove, frankincense, rosemary, ginger and rosewood

Affirmation: "I am safe"

Muladhara is the energy centre at the base of our spine and it connects to our sense of groundedness, as well as to instincts of survival. It also relates to feelings of security, grounding and belonging. When it is out of balance, it causes all the other chakras to be out of balance, because our grounding chakra signifies our survival. When we feel that we are not surviving adequately, we start to compensate in all the other chakras to fix this. As a result we end up with an unbalanced chakra system.

It is important to remember that whenever we work on balancing our chakras, we always start with Muladhara, before proceeding to the other chakras:Svadhisthana, Manipura, Anahata, Vishuddha, Ajna and Sahasrara. Keeping a healthy, solid foundation with Muladhara should be a regular thing in our lives.

There is a vestigial gland at Muladhara chakra which is something like a knot, and this is known as the "knot of Brahma". The energy located in this area is blocked by this knot. In the centre there is a yellow square, which represents the *yantra* (geometrical figure) *Prithvi tattva* (Prithvi = earth; *tattva* = element), the element of Earth and the *bija* mantra LAM. In the centre of the square is a red triangle, which is the symbol of Shakti. Within the triangle is the smoky Swayambhu *linga* (a smooth cylindrical disk-shaped object that symbolizes masculine energy). There is also a serpent, which represents dormant Kundalini (see page 62) and is coiled three and a half times around the *linga*. The triangle is supported by an elephant with seven trunks, which symbolizes seven minerals.

Muladhara is seen as the direct switch that awakens the Ajna chakra. The Annamaya *kosha* (see page 60) sits in this chakra. Muladhara is physiologically related to the excretory, urinary, sexual and reproductive organs.

Muladhara is a chakra that comes off-balance quite easily and constantly, as it represents our physical plane and the material world; and, as imperfect human beings, we live in an imperfect world with all sort of problems and ups and downs. We are still very attached to the material world – to things – and are greatly affected by everything that happens in our world and around us. All the trauma from childhood and past lives is also stored in this chakra. Muladhara is the energy centre that is balancing, transmitting and receiving these energies.

Different States of Muladhara

Blocked Muladhara

This can make us feel restless, with low energy; alienated from ourselves and from others and easily angered. We might have feelings of instability, financial problems, fears and generally feeling ungrounded. Some people experience anxiety and depression, worry and panic, or negative thoughts. On a physical level, with a blocked Muladhara we may experience problems in the colon, lower back pain, leg or feet issues, problems with the bladder, eating disorders and prostate problems.

Open Muladhara

The energy flows freely, making us feel secure, stable, full of health, energy and vitality. We feel grounded, with a sense of belonging and self-worth. We make healthy choices when it comes to food, and we feel firm in our place in life: centred and happy with our lives. When Muladhara is balanced, you find contentment, happiness and inner peace. Some practitioners may experience levitation of the astral body, which is like a sensation of floating upward in space; others experience clairvoyance or clairaudience (hearing something that is inaudible to most people).

Overactive Muladhara

We might be very materialistic and greedy, have a lust for money and power, be aggressive and generally driven by our insecurities when we are not feeling grounded. For example, we may overspend on material things, sometimes spending money that we don't necessarily have, leading to debt and financial troubles.

Underactive Muladhara

We may sense there is a lack of feeling at home or secure anywhere, and be fearful and abandoned. When there is no activation of this chakra there is a lack of connection with your body and your sexuality.

Modern Times and Muladhara

Whether we're experiencing political unrest, a pandemic or a global recession, it is easy to get swept away by the external forces that instil fear and panic on a daily basis, but it is during times like this that we should bring our awareness inward. We are currently going through a global spiritual awakening and this is the time when, more than ever, we need to shift our attention to our bodies and our entire being. We need to bring awareness inward in order to understand what is going on in the external world right now.

These difficult times are perfect for exploring, discussing and learning about our bodies on a more profound level. By discovering the miracles and mysteries that lie under our flesh, we will be able to understand who we truly are and what our true purpose in life is, both as individuals and as a collective. Exploring and learning about the chakras is needed so badly right now, and this knowledge will empower you and help you to navigate the challenges of a rapidly changing world.

Muladhara governs our physical and material world; it is the chakra of foundation and stability in our lives. If we analyse why the collective reacts with fear and in an irrational manner to threat and unrest, we can understand that our basic survival needs are threatened when there is uncertainty around us. People react with a primal instinct to survive by doing whatever they think is the right thing to do. But among the darkness we can see the light of awakening. We can welcome new beginnings, tap into a higher consciousness and increase our self-awareness. We can learn from others, and from our experiences.

There's still a lot of work and healing to do in Muladhara, and this requires a process of purification, cleansing, releasing and detaching. We must raise our vibration and bring awareness into our lives. We depend too much on the material world and need to learn to cherish other people; to trust the universe and God; to move from darkness into the loving light of Anahata chakra.

Think about the next time you are in a fearful situation: How are you going to react? What changes will you make? What will you let go of? What new things will you bring into your life?

Anxiety, fear, stress, depression and insecurities are part of the shadow side of this energy centre. If we wish to heal these ailments, we need to start a Muladhara healing. Grounding meditation, breathing exercises, nature, outdoor activities, yoga and reconnecting with your body are ways to feel grounded and present, rather than being in your mind and worrying about the unknown. Shifting your awareness from the material and physical world toward the spiritual realm is a way to raise your vibration and elevate your consciousness.

Do more research about chakras and the universal process of ascension. Find your tribe, attend healing sessions, be open to receive and learn things beyond the physical reality. All of this can support you during the process of awakening the soul.

Healing Muladhara

The idea of healing your chakras is to bring each chakra alive. It's about embodying and harnessing the energies and bringing them into your life, and using the energy of the chakras to help you live a better life. Below are ten statements regarding Muladhara's qualities. Use them as a self-assessment to help you determine how balanced or unbalanced your Muladhara chakra is at this time. Each statements scores from 1 to 5, with 1 being "I strongly disagree" and 5 "I strongly agree". If you score 10, you have a balanced Muladhara chakra: congratulations! If you score over 10 you are showing symptoms of an unbalanced chakra. The higher the score, the more blocked your Muladhara is. Incorporating Muladhara healing exercises and using the knowledge in this book can help you release the blockages that are present in this chakra and therefore increase the flow of *prana* in this energy centre.

1. I generally feel scared and insecure
2. I normally find it difficult to let go of past emotions and experiences
3. I have sciatica or lower-back pain
4. I experience problems with my legs and/or feet
5. I regularly have bowel problems/feel constipated
6. I normally feel I don't have enough energy throughout the day
7. I feel a low connection with the Earth
8. I don't feel much connection with my body
9. I have low libido
10. I feel like I constantly have financial problems and work worries

Muladhara healing is the practice of stimulating, opening, cleansing and strengthening this first chakra. Here you will find a series of exercises, tips and healing techniques for Muladhara balancing. To get the best out of them and positive results, try and do them for at least three or four continuous days. Use the food, crystals, sound, colours, positive affirmations, meditation and yoga poses described to balance and strengthen this energy centre. Incorporate them in your daily life.

Yoga Poses for Muladhara

Add these postures to your yoga practice, or even as part of your exercise routine.

- Vrikshasana (Tree Pose)
- Savasana (Corpse Pose)
- Malasana (yoga squat)
- Balasana (Child's Pose)
- Virabhadrasana II (Warrior II)
- Janu Sirsasana (Head-to-Knee Forward Bend)
- Sukhasana (Easy Pose)

Nourishment for Muladhara

Add as much red food to your diet as you like during Muladhara healing. For example, add red berries to your breakfast cereal, and use red tomatoes and red peppers in your salads. Eat earthy food, like red potatoes and sweet potatoes. And enjoy red fruits throughout the day. Try to eat fresh and natural, and avoid processed food.

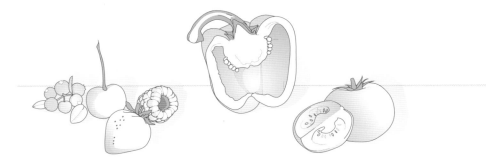

Meditation

Duration: 3–5 minutes, or as long as you wish

1. Sit in a cross-legged position or on a chair, then bring your awareness to Muladhara chakra.

2. Breathe into Muladhara, visualizing expansion of the colour red as you inhale and exhale.

3. You can apply essential oils on your pulse points, play music for Muladhara or do this meditation chanting the *bija* mantra LAM. Repeat some positive affirmations for this chakra (see page 285).

Mudra for Muladhara: Jnana *Mudra*

Duration: 5 minutes

1. Sit in a cross-legged position or on a chair. Rest both hands on your knees, facing upward.

2. Join the tip of your index finger with the tip of your thumb. Meditate on this *mudra* for 5 minutes.

Muladhara Zen Moments

Cultivate the habit of reconnecting with Muladhara regularly. Try taking a walk outside in nature, reconnecting with the soil and the Earth – achieving Zen moments that are guided by intuition rather than by conscious effort. Be grateful for all your blessings, and focus on what you have rather than what is lacking in your life. And if there's something missing from your life, work toward it and remember that you have the ability to create your own reality.

Here are some suggestions to help you reconnect with Muladhara:
- Spend some time in nature
- Walk around the house in bare feet
- Dance some tribal music
- Wear the colour red
- Sit on the floor
- Stamp your feet and feel the ground beneath you
- Plant some flowers
- Hug trees
- Have wooden items around you

"I am grounded. This is my land and I belong here. I have everything I need to build the life I want."

Second Chakra: Svadhisthana or Sacral Chakra

SVADHISTHANA ASSOCIATIONS
Name: *Sva* = self; *Sthan* = dwelling place
Qualities: Creativity, sexuality, sensuality, procreation, emotions, sensations, flexibility, expression, relationships, connections, pleasure, movement
Location: Pelvic area under the pubic bone, about 7.5cm (3in) below the belly button; the sacral plexus
Organs/systems: Ovaries, genitals, bladder, kidney, womb, bowel, lower intestine; reproductive system, urinary system
Endocrine glands: Adrenal glands, ovaries and testicle glands
Colour: Orange
Flower: Six petals
Element: Water
Deities: Vishnu, Rakini, Mata Saraswati
Mantra: VAM
Sense: Taste
Sensory organ: Tongue
Organs of activity: Sexual organs
Animal: *Makara* (sea dragon in Hindu mythology)
Food: Oranges, carrots, pumpkins, mandarins, apricots, mangoes, peaches, papayas, flax seeds, sweet potatoes, lentils, beans, almonds, orange peppers, honey, coconuts
Musical note: D
Crystals: Carnelian, orange calcite, amber, orange aventurine, tiger's eye, sunstone, agate, copper, aragonite
Essential oils: Cardamom, chamomile, ylang-ylang, eucalyptus, patchouli, rose, clary sage
Affirmation: "I am creative"

Svadhisthana is the energy centre located at the navel. It is associated with the emotions and creativity, and helps us form our creative expressions. It also helps us to be open to intimacy while being passionate and lively. People with a healthy, open Svadhisthana are passionate, present in their body, sensual, creative and connected to their feelings. Svadhisthana is associated with the unconscious and is closely related to the first chakra, Muladhara. If Muladhara is blocked or out of balance, this will impact tremendously on Svadhisthana, almost by default. Basically, because they are so connected with each other, you can't have one without the other: you can't enjoy the pleasures of life if your basic needs aren't covered. It's as simple as that.

This chakra is symbolized by a lotus with six petals. It is a chakra for the Water element, so the *bija* mantra is VAM. The *yantra* is constituted for a crescent moon, and the *bija* mantra is shown riding on a crocodile that symbolizes the movements of the karmas. Karma means "action" or "deed" and refers to the spiritual principle that the actions of an individual influence their future. Do good, and good will come to you; do bad, and bad will come to you. That's karma.

The Svadhisthana chakra seeks pleasure and security. It's associated with the taste/tongue and the genitals. Svadhisthana is the seat of the individual and collective unconscious. Feeling stuck in life, that there is not much happening and there is not much flow – this could be a sign of Svadhisthana being blocked. When this chakra is open and balanced our life flows: we flow with these energies, just like water; and if there's an obstacle on the way, water adapts easily and continues its course. This is when we need to bring awareness to this chakra and work on it to dissolve stagnation.

Different States of Svadhisthana

Blocked Svadhisthana

This can make us have a low libido and feel repressed from expressing our emotions; we may experience emotional instability, jealousy, guilt, sexual dysfunction or addictions. We might experience possessiveness or shame of our body/sexuality. On a physical level, the blockage of Svadhisthana can cause bladder problems, frigidity, gall and kidney stones and pelvic issues, among other problems.

Open Svadhisthana

We will experience feelings like joy, pleasure, sexuality, sensuality, nurturing and procreation, and deep emotions like passion and optimism. An open and balanced Svadhisthana is important for living a balanced, healthy and prosperous life.

Overactive Svadhisthana

We will be over-emotional or feel emotional all the time, will be attracted to drama and will feel emotionally attached to people. We may be moody, lacking personal boundaries and very sexual. Usually there are no healthy intentions behind our actions.

Underactive Svadhisthana

This detaches us from our emotions and from those around us, and gives us an inability to cope with life changes. We may have a desire to self-destruct, abusive relationships, be easily manipulated or controlled and have very little confidence and self-esteem.

Modern Times and Svadhisthana

How many times have you heard the phrase "the feminine rising" or "the divine feminine"? If you are on the spiritual path, I'm sure you have heard it very frequently, especially in the last few years. The divine feminine is definitely on the rise, and I'm a vivid example of it, as I will share with you later on.

First, I want to mention briefly something important about this chakra. When talking about Svadhisthana, we think of it as the centre of the energy of creation and manifestation. Remember also that the element of this chakra is Water, and where there is water there is life. Human life is created in the woman's womb. Whether you have a physical womb or not, you are linked to it through your mother's womb. Svadhisthana is located about 7.5cm (3in) below the navel area; and in women it is located at the bottom of the womb. When you are born into the physical world, you are energetically and physically attached to your mother's womb and bring with you some of your mother's womb-energy.

So when you think about it, we are all here in this lifetime holding our own energy and the energy of our ancestors, given to us when we were conceived. And we also have an energetically strong attachment to our mother's womb, because that's where we came from. The womb is a sacred space; it's the container of new life, which is a miracle and a manifestation of the universe. It is in fact the universe itself manifesting in physical form. And women are sacred for being the vehicle that enables this divine manifestation of love to happen.

In our current troubled times, men and women have in a way lost the connection with this sacred space. Women are not connected with their own wombs, and men are completely detached from that space as they get older. The call has gone out to reconnect with it, make peace with it and acknowledge and honour this sacred space.

During my Kundalini course, before we started to cover the Svadhisthana chakra, we were all (both men and women aspirants) required to receive a womb-healing session. This was extremely healing on the physical, emotional and spiritual levels. One of the parts I enjoyed most was imaging using the Water element: visualizing the ocean's waters washing my mother's womb and my own. This felt so healing and liberating. We were made to visit this sacred space again on a quantum level, as adults, and once all the healing was done, we were reborn into this life from a healed and cleansed womb. My relationship with myself as a woman has now changed; and my relationship with my mother, sisters and other women has changed, too, since this beautiful acknowledgement of the woman's womb. My creativity has shifted, my relationship with my own physical body and my sensuality is a lot better, and I feel I can express myself better now. I have allowed myself to flow through life, just like water.

This experience is just a little part of a huge movement happening right now within the collective. The divine feminine is rising, and women are coming together to reclaim our inner power. Women are the physical manifestation of *shakti*, the powerful feminine energy of creation and manifestation that lies within our being. Men and women hold aspects of both masculine and feminine energies, but the feminine energy is dormant in Muladhara. However, by reclaiming our inner power, doing self-healing, connecting with our sensuality, honouring and embodying who we are and reconnecting with the womb-space, we are creating the space for the divine feminine to rise.

When I say "reclaiming our inner power" I mean the feminine energy, which is both consciously and unconsciously suppressed and devalued by men and women. We live in a very competitive world dominated by men, so the masculine energy in our bodies is overpowering the feminine energy, and this is what we can see manifesting in the world. For the past thousand years we have lived in a world that has largely been led by men: conquering, using logical thinking, rationality, power and physical strength – all masculine qualities. On the other side, the feminine-energy qualities are nature, intuition, compassion, flexibility, healing, expression and nurturing.

If we want to save the world, and ourselves, we must rebalance these two energies. We must take a look at our lives with an honest and creative approach, observe the areas that are out of balance and realign them with our true self and for the highest good. By tapping into feminine-energy qualities, we can be open to receive this cosmic energy and manifest it not only in our lives, but out in the world, where it is so badly needed.

The ways that I started tapping into the feminine energy were by researching, self-study, connecting with others already on this path, doing healing sessions, tapping into my intuition and creativity, expressing myself, being inspired by art, music, dancing and moving. Svadhisthana is about moving and being flexible in all aspects of your life; practising yoga; and giving yourself permission to both give and receive pleasure from a place of love and integrity.

Healing Svadhisthana

The idea of healing your chakras is to bring each chakra alive. It's about embodying and harnessing the energies and bringing them into your life, and using the energy of the chakras to help you live a better life.

Here are ten statements regarding Svadhisthana's qualities. Use them as a self-assessment to help you determine how balanced or unbalanced your Svadhisthana chakra is at this time. Each statements scores from 1 to 5, with 1 being "I strongly disagree" and 5 "I strongly agree". If you score 10, you have a balanced Svadhisthana chakra: congratulations! If you score over 10 you are showing symptoms of an unbalanced chakra. The higher the score, the more blocked your Svadhisthana is. Incorporating Svadhisthana healing exercises and using the knowledge in this book can help you release the blockages that are present in this chakra and therefore increase the flow of *prana* in this energy centre.

1. I find difficult to let go of negative emotions
2. I have a tendency toward addictive behaviour
3. I feel my sexuality is blocked or have a lack of sexual drive
4. Sometimes I have feelings of guilt, jealousy and shame
5. I am ashamed of my body
6. I have issues with my reproductive system
7. I usually have lower-back problems
8. I feel my creativity is stuck
9. I have a tendency to be involved in toxic relationships
10. I have stiff hips/restrictions in this part of my body

Svadhisthana healing is the practice of stimulating, opening, cleansing and strengthening this chakra. Get the most out of the exercises, tips and healing techniques explained here by doing them for at least three or four continuous days. Use the food, crystals, sound, colours, positive affirmations, meditation and yoga mentioned – basically everything that is related to this chakra – to cleanse and strengthen this energy centre. A lot of energy and inner-child healing take place in the womb-space, and emotional trauma tends to store in the area of the reproductive organs and around the hips.

Yoga Poses for Svadhisthana

A hip-focused yoga practice can release discomfort and stuck energies.

- Utkata Konasana (Goddess Pose)
- Eka Pada Rajakapotasana (Pigeon Pose)
- Mandukasana (Frog Pose)
- Padottanasana C (Wide-legged Forward Bend C)
- Utthita Balasana (Extended Child's Pose)
- Ashwa Sanchalanasana (Low Lunge)

Nourishment for Svadhisthana

The food related to this chakra contains the colour orange: so oranges, orange peppers, pumpkins, papayas and sweet potatoes. By making sure that you have a balanced diet you can also maintain balanced chakras. Observe what is lacking in your daily diet. What colours of the rainbow are missing from your plate? Food is our source of energy, so pay attention to the quality of the food you eat. Keep your body hydrated: drink plenty of fluids.

Meditation

Duration: 3–5 minutes

1. Sit in a cross-legged position or on a chair, then bring your awareness to Svadhisthana chakra.

2. Breathe into Svadhisthana, visualizing expansion of the colour orange as you inhale and exhale.

3. You can apply essential oils on your pulse points, play music for Svadhisthana or do this meditation chanting the *bija* mantra VAM. Repeat some positive affirmations for this chakra (see page 286).

Mudra for Svadhisthana: Dhyani *Mudra*

Duration: 5 minutes

1. Sit in a cross-legged position or on a chair. Rest your right hand on top of your left hand, with the palms facing up and the tips of the thumbs touching each other.

2. Place this *mudra* at the Svadhisthana level of your body. Meditate on this *mudra* for 5 minutes.

Svadhisthana Zen Moments

Cultivate the habit of reconnecting with Svadhisthana regularly. Twice a week
I like to practise chakra dance (see page 228), whether as a self-practice or by
joining local groups. It feels very liberating, refreshing and the sense of
reconnecting with my body, honouring and embodying my sensuality, is important
to me. Remember: no one should feel ashamed of their body, and as long as you
execute activities from a place of love and integrity, they are safe. Whatever you
choose to do, try to achieve some Zen moments that are guided by intuition rather
than by conscious effort.

Here are some suggestions to help you reconnect with Svadhisthana:
- Spend some time near water
- Swim
- Do some tribal dance with a water sound-effect
- Wear the colour orange
- Encourage the flow of creativity by doing something that requires
  imagination, such as drawing, painting or decorating
- Soak in a warm bath
- Surround yourself with art and creativity

"I am like water, always flexible, shapeless and in movement. Everything in me flows."

Third Chakra: Manipura or Solar Plexus Chakra

MANIPURA ASSOCIATIONS

Name: *Mani* = jewel/gem; *Pura* = place, city

Qualities: Confidence, self-esteem, self-worth, self-control, willpower, calmness, initiative, a "can do" attitude, discipline

Location: 5–7.5cm (2–3in) above the belly button at the base of the ribcage; the solar plexus

Organs/systems: Stomach, upper abdomen, metabolism, upper intestines, upper back, spine, liver, gall bladder; digestive system, endocrine system

Endocrine glands: Pancreas, outer adrenal glands, gastric glands

Colour: Yellow

Flower: Ten petals

Element: Fire

Deities: Rudra, Lakini

Mantra: RAM

Sense: Sight

Sensory organ: Eyes

Organ of activity: Feet

Animal: Ram or billy goat

Food: Squash, beans, bananas, yellow peppers, brown rice, pineapples, lemons, corn, ginger, turmeric, butternut squash, oats, peaches, apricots

Musical note: E

Crystals: Citrine, yellow sapphire, amber, tiger's eye, yellow jasper, lemon quartz, peridot, yellow labradorite

Essential oils: Sandalwood, cinnamon, ginger, saffron, musk, orange, lemongrass, grapefruit, lemon, eucalyptus

Affirmation: "I am strong"

This chakra is the centre of your vitality, and is also called the power or Sun chakra. It represents the core of your personality, identity and ego. The energy of Manipura allows you to move forward in life in a balanced manner. Harnessing the energies of this chakra means being active rather than inactive, and going through life with confidence, drive and a strong sense of life. When our consciousness has reached Manipura, we have overcome the negative aspects and challenges of Svadhisthana. This chakra acts like a little magnet in our bodies, attracting *prana* from the cosmos, receiving it in and distributing the energy to the other chakras, just like the Sun in our solar system – hence the colour of this chakra is bright yellow, symbolizing the Sun within ourselves.

Manipura is represented as a bright-yellow lotus with ten petals. Within the lotus is a red triangle, the *yantra* of *agni tattva*, the Fire element, and the *bija* mantra RAM. This energy centre oversees the vital processes of digestion and food metabolism. It governs the functioning of the gastric glands, the gall bladder, pancreas and other organs that produce the necessary enzymes for good digestion and the absorption of nutrients. When there are blockages in Manipura, these manifest usually as stomach or digestive issues.

A lot of people believe that our intuition is located only in Ajna chakra, but Manipura also plays an important role in intuition and, more specifically, our guts. This is what the expression "Listen to your gut" refers to. If something or someone does not feel right, then Manipura will pick up on those energies, sending signals to our body, making us feel unsure or alert about it. That first instinct is due to the exchange of energies between our bodies and everything around us.

Emotions are also felt in this energy centre and can impact physically on the organs, glands and system related to it. The best way to explain this is to think about a time when you were really sad; this feeling was probably felt in your abdomen, resulting in a loss of appetite. And if you were very excited about something, perhaps you lost your appetite as well. Your Manipura has absorbed and processed those strong energies, and as it controls the digestive system, this will be the first area in your physical body where the emotions will be felt.

This chakra is all about being able to deal with things. It is not only about how you digest food, but also about how you digest the sweet and the sour in life.

Different States of Manipura

Blocked Manipura

If this occurs, we have feelings of low self-esteem, powerlessness, submissiveness and an inferiority complex. We might feel the world is against us or that we just can't get ahead in life or with our projects. A blocked Manipura can not only affect us on the emotional level, but also on the physical level; for example, with diabetes, ulcers, liver and colon disease, eating disorders, digestive/stomach problems, back pain, lethargy and gas.

Open Manipura

If we have an open Manipura, that means we have drive and confidence. We have a great self-image, feel like we are in control and have willpower and assertiveness. There is no self-doubt, we are more decisive. We feel empowered and confident. As we claim our power we don't feel anxious or stressed, we feel more calmed. We don't experience digestive system disorders. We eat healthily and only what our bodies need for survival. We feel full of vitality and are flexible in the navel area.

Overactive Manipura

We might find ourselves judging people too harshly or becoming too critical and demanding. We may display anger and aggressiveness, overpowering others with a false display of confidence, or we might be manipulative.

Underactive Manipura

We tend to be passive and indecisive, and probably feel powerless and ineffective. It is difficult to accomplish tasks, being riddled with self-doubt. We may have an inactive, "I can't be bothered" attitude. There is no sparkle, fire or passion.

Modern Times and Manipura

Our navels are getting exposed to the world – and I don't mean that literally. I mean that our emotions are becoming exposed, and I am referring to the way we, as individuals and nations, are managing our emotions. This is an important part in the spiritual awakening process. We are working consciously and unconsciously in our navel chakra. We have been guided to become more aware of our emotions, and have been shown different ways that we can express them and cope with them. We are finally realizing how important it is to acknowledge our emotions rather than brush them under the carpet. We are more open and ready to talk about uncomfortable topics. We are healing and, in the process, we must bring awareness to the self and the ego. There is an increase in light-workers and healers guiding those who seek healing and spiritual awakening. Manipura is the site for our emotions. If we have a chakra that is cluttered with old emotions and energy blockages, how are we supposed to open to receive the new energy into our body that is necessary for our energy body?

On the physical level, Manipura controls the stomach and digestive system, and during stressful times, our lifestyle, diet and the strength of our immune system are exposed. We realize that our immune system (also found in our guts) is not as strong as we thought and we won't necessarily be able to fight off infection.

People are more aware now of what they put in their mouths, and there is an increase in the number of vegetarians and vegans around the world. People enjoy cooking fresh food and are more conscious now of the importance of living a healthy lifestyle. The Manipura chakra not only processes and digests everything that we put in our mouths, but also the emotions and feelings that we have to swallow in our lifetime. All those are old energies and have to be released.

The silver lining of any stressful situation is the dissolving of ego, the awakening of Manipura, the realization of the self, awareness of our wellbeing and lifestyle, and many other beautiful things that we see as a result of such circumstances. Working with Manipura requires a lot of navel work, yoga *asanas* and *kriyas* that stimulate this energy centre, as well as *pranayama* for purifying and detoxifying physically, mentally and emotionally. We can use the mantras and *mudras* to activate this chakra, and therefore to activate the *agni* (fire) within us.

Healing Manipura

The idea of healing your chakras is to bring each chakra alive. It's about embodying and harnessing the energies and bringing them into your life, and using the energy of the chakras to help you live a better life.

Here are ten statements regarding Manipura's qualities. Use them as a self-assessment to help you determine how balanced or unbalanced your Manipura chakra is at this time. Each statements scores from 1 to 5, with 1 being "I strongly disagree" and 5 "I strongly agree". If you score 10, you have a balanced Manipura chakra: congratulations! If you score over 10 you are showing symptoms of an unbalanced chakra. The higher the score, the more blocked your Manipura is. Incorporating Manipura healing exercises and using the knowledge in this book can help you release the blockages that are present in this chakra and therefore increase the flow of *prana* in this energy centre.

1. I don't feel empowered, strong and confident
2. I find it difficult to feel worthy of success, happiness and love
3. I struggle taking responsibility for my actions
4. I feel powerless to manifest my dreams and desires
5. I give up easily – I don't chase my dreams
6. I don't think I am totally responsible for my emotions
7.   I don't always feel motivated to achieve my goals
8. I normally have digestive/stomach problems
9. I lack of energy most of the time
10. I feel like I am in constant competition with others

Manipura healing is the practice of awakening, opening, cleansing and strengthening the chakra. To heal Manipura, focus on doing the exercises, tips and healing techniques described here for at least three or four continuous days. Use the food, crystals, sound, colours, positive affirmations, meditation, yoga mentioned – basically everything that is related to this chakra – to cleanse, and strengthen this energy centre. It is so important to keep eye on Manipura, because any imbalances may compromise your gut health and affect your emotional and mental wellbeing. The gut is often considered a second brain due to its constant communication with the brain. It is said that when this energy centre is purified and awakened, the body becomes disease-free and radiant.

Yoga Poses for Manipura

Backbends, twists and *pranayama* are great to cleanse and awaken this chakra.

- Setu Bandha Sarvangasana (Bridge Pose)
- Chakrasana (Wheel Pose)
- Ustrasana (Camel Pose)
- Kapalabhati *pranayama*
- Adho Mukha Svanasana (Downward-facing Dog)
- Parvritta Trikonasana (Revolved Triangle)
- Balasana (Child's Pose)
- Bhujangasana (Cobra Pose)
- Navasana (Boat Pose)

Nourishment for Manipura

The foods related to this chakra contain the colour yellow: bananas, yellow peppers, pineapples, potatoes, corn, mangoes, cauliflowers, peaches, apricots and lemons. Embrace the colour yellow and bring a little bit of Sun into your life. By making sure you have a balanced diet you can also maintain a balanced chakra. Observe what is lacking in your daily diet. What colours of the rainbow are missing from your plate? Food is our source of energy, so pay attention to the quality of food you eat. And always opt for fresh natural food.

Meditation

1. Sit in a cross-legged position or on a chair, then bring your awareness to Manipura chakra.

2. Breathe into Manipura, visualizing expansion of the colour yellow as you inhale and exhale.

3. You can apply essential oils on your pulse points, play music for Manipura or do this meditation chanting the *bija* mantra. Repeat some positive affirmations for this chakra (see page 287).

Mudra for Manipura: Hakini *Mudra*

1. Sit in a cross-legged position or on a chair. Bring all your fingertips together, with the thumbs against each other, forming a triangle.

2. Place this *mudra* at Manipura or your navel centre, with the fingers projecting upward. Meditate on this *mudra* for a while. You can also chant the *bija* mantra RAM.

You can also perform this mudra on the Ajna chakra. Practising this stimulates the brain and balances the energy flow between both sides of the body and the two sides of the brain.

Manipura Zen Moments

Cultivate the habit of reconnecting with Manipura regularly. Be proud of who you are and what you have achieved in life. Everyone has different struggles and we are all walking different paths. Be gentle and kind to yourself, and make sure you take care of your physical body. Whatever you choose to do, try to achieve some Zen moments that are guided by intuition rather than by conscious effort.

Here are some suggestions to help you reconnect with Manipura:
- Do some journaling
- Spend time in the sunshine
- Light candles and meditate
- Enjoy a sauna
- Wear the colour yellow
- Practise one day of fasting once or twice a month
- Work on your projects – do some mind-mapping

"I have all the energy, inner power and self-confidence I need to achieve my goals while helping others to achieve theirs, too."

Fourth Chakra: Anahata or Heart Chakra

ANAHATA ASSOCIATIONS
Name: *Anahata* = unhurt, unstruck, unbeaten
Qualities: Peace, bliss, harmony, empathy, clarity, purity, love, understanding, unity, compassion, kindness, forgiveness
Location: Behind the centre of the chest
Organs/systems: Heart, lungs, arms, hands; immune system, respiratory system
Endocrine gland: Thymus gland (immunity)
Colour: Green
Flower: 12 petals
Element: Air
Deities: Isha, Kakini
Mantra: YAM
Sense: Touch
Sensory organ: Skin
Organ of activity: Hands
Animal: Antelope
Food: Kale, broccoli, spinach, celery, cucumbers, avocadoes, courgettes, limes, matcha tea, green tea, kiwi fruit, peas, wheatgrass, mint, green beans, lettuce
Musical note: F
Crystals: Jade, peridot, rose quartz, green aventurine, emerald, malachite
Essential oils: Jasmine, rose, marjoram, chamomile, mandarin, melissa, lavender, geranium
Affirmation: "I am love"

Anahata is the energy centre and is associated with consciousness and spirituality. It embodies our ability to love unconditionally. This chakra is considered to be where the soul is seated. Anahata is very powerful as it holds the highest vibration of the universe: "Love". The energy of this chakra radiates out of the heart to the lungs, chest and into the arms and hands, so that our soul can express itself, communicate and help others in the physical world.

Remember: this is a spiritual chakra, so if you direct this energy toward desired objects and lower-self elements, then you tend to have an affinity with those objects, which can lead to material delusion. However, Anahata is able to neutralize and transmute those energies into divine love. The energies of this chakra should always be used in a positive way, and our actions should match our true intentions.

It is important to bring balance into our lives, as well as to achieve balance in our emotions. Life can sometimes be challenging, and this is when we most need to keep a check on our chakras in order to maintain a good balance in our emotions, which will ultimately become actions in our lives.

The word Anahata means "unstruck". All sound in the universe is produced by striking together at least two objects that produce vibrations or sound. However, the primordial sound that originates beyond this material world is the *Anahata nada* (the unstruck sound).

This chakra is represented by a lotus flower with 12 petals. In the centre of the lotus is a hexagon with two interlacing triangles. This is the *yantra* of the Air element. The *bija* mantra is YAM, and Anahata's animal is an antelope.

The more you operate from the lower chakras (Muladhara, Svadhisthana and Manipura), the more you will remain dependent on what is already enjoined for you – your fate or destiny. This is called *prarabdha karma*. Only when you overcome the challenges of these three chakras and shift your consciousness to the higher chakras can you reach Anahata and become a yogi. As a yogi, you depend solely on the power of your own consciousness rather than on anything that is external. Tantra traditions say that at the root of Anahata there is a wish-fulfilling tree and when this tree starts to fructify, whatever you think or wish comes true. This tree is known as *kalpa taru* or *kalpa vriksha*.

Symptoms of opening or awakening Anahata show that you are becoming more aware of this part of your body and are bringing more attention to it. You are becoming more sensitive to life and experiences. You feel an immense sense of love and fulfilment. You feel open to give and receive. Anahata is associated with the heart, lungs, arms, respiratory and circulatory systems. It is believed that the soul lives just below the heart space, under the left ribcage.

Different States of Anahata

Blocked Anahata

If Anahata is blocked, we may feel emotionally unstable and sad, with an inability to love and share, a lack of self-love, jealousy, a sense of abandonment, envy, rejection, bitterness and fear. On the physical level, a blocked heart chakra can impact on the lungs and respiratory system, presenting problems such as asthma, allergies, a weak immune system, heart issues, aches in the chest, hypertension, pneumonia and circulatory issues.

Open Anahata

If we have an open heart chakra, we feel compassion for others, inner peace, satisfaction and are able to share and love unconditionally. We practise self-love, unity and gratitude. We promote harmony and respect to self and others. We feel joy and fulfilment, and have stable relationships.

Overactive Anahata

If this occurs, we might be loving in a suffocating way, lacking boundaries, letting everyone in, and feeling bitterness, jealousy, anger, fear or loneliness. We might be attached to our relationships, putting others before ourselves and unable to find independence.

Underactive Anahata

We tend to be cold, distant, feel low and have negative thoughts. We find it hard to connect with others and to forgive, and exhibit selfish behaviour.

Modern Times and Anahata

I have always thought that our responsibility as individuals is to cherish our society and the planet. I have had strong ideas that I must do something remarkable and belong to a movement to save the planet – or whatever is needed in the world. All these superhero and activist ideas were changed when, in a lecture one day with my guru, he told us, "We didn't come to this life to save the world; we came to this life to save ourselves. When we take care of ourselves properly, the world will take care of itself."

So simple and so true. We cannot love others, our parents, our family, our friends, the planet and the animals if we don't understand and love ourselves first. Pure love starts within, and only once we totally harness and embody the energies of self-love can we go around spreading love.

First of all, what is love to you? What actually is love: what does it mean? You will answer according to what you think love is, because that's what you have experienced; another person will answer something different, based on their own feelings and experiences; and someone else will answer something different again; and so on… Everyone has an idea of what love is, although no one has seen it, but has only experienced what we think love is.

We try to attach things to the concept, but the reality is that love could be anything and has different meanings for different people. For instance, if I'm holding a pen and I ask one hundred people what the name of the object that I'm holding is, then one hundred people will answer that it is a pen, and nothing else needs to be said. Everyone agrees that it is a pen, and I will be satisfied with that answer because I know it is a pen.

If I ask one hundred people, "What is love?" I will get one hundred different answers, so which one is the truth? If, for instance, I agree with someone who says that a mother's feeling for her child is love, maybe someone in the crowd will say that her mother abandoned or abused her when she was a child; then we have two different opinions, and we realize that love was present for some and not for others. But pure love doesn't work like that. Do you understand my point? Love is equally for everyone, and it starts within ourselves.

Love cannot be described, but only felt when we love ourselves. Love is God, the divine, the universe, the almighty, unity and the supreme energy of the universe. More than ever now, we need lots of love in this world, but most importantly we need first to open our heart centre to receive and accept love in ourselves.

When you compare yourself to others, you are not loving yourself. When you are not nourishing your body with the right food, you are not loving yourself. When you hold anger toward others, you are not loving yourself. When you smoke, you are not loving yourself. When you are having negative thoughts toward yourself or others, you are not loving yourself. When you continue working and working non-stop, you are not loving yourself... And I could go on, because the list is endless.

Self-love isn't just about having a bubble bath, sitting for 30 minutes in meditation or attending your yoga class. Self-love is way more than that. It's about self-acceptance and surrender, letting go of whatever is holding you back and taking you away from the present moment. Self-love is about letting go of attachments, labels, titles and ego, so that you can enter the heart-space as a pure soul. To me, self-love starts with detachment from everything that is not in alignment with your true self. That has to be the first step in the process. But how ready are you to let go of the material and physical? How ready are you to let go of the labels, status and ego?

As a civilization, we are still healing and overcoming the negative qualities and challenges of the first three lower chakras (the chakras of matter), and we are going from Muladhara to Manipura, and back again, in circles. These chakras are the ones that control and represent the 3D world in which we live, because everything that is happening internally within our energy centres is also represented in our reality. When we are ready to step into the 5D world we will be ascending to Anahata (the spiritual chakra) – the chakra of pure divine love and light that cleanses the soul, before stepping into the other spiritual chakras. If we are stuck in the lower chakras, we can't simply ascend to higher-frequency energies. When we move to Anahata as a collective – probably in many, many lifetimes to come – we will live in a different world, without chaos and disease, without wars and fights, competitions and ego. It will be a world of unconditional love, equality, compassion, kindness and gratitude.

So how can we move forward, as a collective and as spiritual beings, into these higher dimensions? How can we start this process? How can we make a change so that our world changes? These are probably some of the questions you will be asking yourself right now. The universal ascension process has already started, and we are all going through it. The planet is slowly ascending to a higher vibration and, with it, we are going too, whether we like it or not. So we need to bring awareness not only to our physical world, but also to our spiritual world. We have to stop searching outward and delve within. We need to be more of the spiritual beings that we are, and less of the human beings.

Journaling and meditating, asking questions such as "Who am I?", are a good start; as is letting go of all the material stuff that we don't need any more. We tend to accumulate more and more stuff, and sometimes we become so greedy that we are never satisfied – but these things we need to learn to let go of. We need to cultivate a practice of self-love every day, and by this I mean connecting with the divine, with your Higher Self, asking for guidance and support to be open to God, letting it shower your entire being with light and love. Practise gratitude every day. Let go of anything that is disturbing your inner peace – that's self-love.

When you practise these things regularly, you are shifting toward the Higher Self, and you will naturally think, speak, see, hear and feel only love. You will become love yourself. Self-love is about detaching from the Lower Self, from ego and this flesh that we think we are. This body is an avatar that carries our soul, allowing the soul to experience this physical world. However, the labels, names, professions and titles don't belong to the soul, and the soul doesn't need or want them – in fact the soul wants to be liberated from them. The soul lives under the heart, below the ribcage on the left side of your body.

Anahata governs the lungs and the respiratory system. On a spiritual level, when our lungs and breathing are attacked by disease and infection, this is bringing our attention to this chakra. It is a call that we need to work on Anahata and the Spirit that lives within it. So although I agree that we need to take care of our planet, our oceans and other people, my main message is that we need to take care of ourselves first, by nourishing and honouring our soul.

Healing Anahata

The idea of healing your chakras is to bring each chakra alive. It's about embodying and harnessing the energies and bringing them into your life, and using the energy of the chakras to help you live a better life.

Here are ten statements regarding Anahata's qualities. Use them as a self-assessment to help you determine how balanced or unbalanced your Anahata chakra is at this time. Each statements scores from 1 to 5, with 1 being "I strongly disagree" and 5 being "I strongly agree". If you score 10, you have a balanced Anahata chakra: congratulations! If you score over 10 you are showing symptoms of an unbalanced chakra. The higher the score, the more blocked your Anahata is. Incorporating Anahata healing exercises and using the knowledge in this book can help you release the blockages that are present in this chakra and therefore increase the flow of *prana* in this energy centre.

1. I have problems showing self-love
2. I don't easily forget what others did to me
3. I normally don't feel compassion and sympathy for others
4. I usually forget to be grateful for my blessings
5. I feel rejected by others
6. I have heart problems
7. I have respiratory and lung problems
8. I find it difficult to forgive
9. I am normally a jealous person
10. Most of my relationships aren't honest and sincere

Anahata healing is the practice of stimulating, awakening, opening, cleansing and strengthening this chakra. To heal Anahata, follow the exercises, tips and healing techniques described here and the knowledge shared in this book. Try to focus on Anahata healing at least for three or four continuous days. Use the food, crystals, sound, colours, positive affirmations, meditation and yoga mentioned – basically everything that is related to this chakra – to cleanse and strengthen this energy centre. When Anahata awakens, you are opening a new world of incredible possibilities, because this is the chakra where your thoughts and desires are materialized and fulfilled.

Yoga Poses for Anahata

I love Camel Pose and any chest-opening poses to cleanse Anahata and promote self-healing.

- Ustrasana (Camel Pose)
- Chkrasana (Wheel Pose)
- Setu Bandha Sarvangasana (Bridge Pose)
- Bhujangasana (Cobra Pose)
- Urdhva Mukha Svanasana (Upward-facing Dog)
- Dhanurasana (Bow Pose)
- Camatkarasana (Wild Thing Pose)

Nourishment for Anahata

Eat all the fresh greens that are available to you, including broccoli, spinach, green beans, lettuces, kale, limes, cucumber, courgettes, green peppers, kiwis and green apples. Drink herbal teas, green tea, peppermint tea, matcha tea and green smoothies. Food associated with Anahata is vegan or plant-based, light, fresh, organic, green and soft. Avoid too much spice.

Meditation

Duration: 5 minutes, or as long as you wish

1. Sit in a cross-legged position or on a chair. Find a quite place, close your eyes and bring your awareness to Anahata.

2. Breathe into Anahata, visualizing expansion of the colour green as you inhale and exhale.

3. You can apply essential oils on your pulse points, play music for Anahata or do this meditation chanting the *bija* mantra YAM while meditating. Repeat some positive affirmations for this chakra as well (see page 288).

Mudra for Anahata: Padma *Mudra*

Duration: 3–5 minutes

1. Sitting with crossed legs or on a chair, bring both hands in front of your chest at Anahata level.

2. Join the fingertips of the little fingers and thumbs together, and the base of both hands, creating the shape of an open lotus flower. Meditate on this *mudra* for a while. Close your eyes and stay here for few minutes as you breathe in and out of your Anahata chakra.

Anahata Zen Moments

Stimulate and activate this chakra by being kind to everyone, and any living thing on this planet. Do it in such a way that everyone who comes into contact with you sees those qualities in you. If each of us brought awareness to Anahata and what it is asking us to do, our lives would be happier and healthier, and so would our world. Whatever you choose to do, try to achieve some Zen moments that are guided by intuition rather than by conscious effort.

Here are some suggestions to help you reconnect with Anahata:
- Gently massage the centre of your chest
- Wear the colour green
- Spend time with your loved ones
- Play with your pets
- Practise gratitude
- Practise forgiveness
- Practise self-love
- Do something that makes your soul happy

"My heart only radiates kindness, compassion, forgiveness and unconditional love. What my heart gives my heart receives."

Fifth Chakra: Vishuddha or Throat Chakra

VISHUDDHA ASSOCIATIONS

Name: *Vishuddha* = especially pure/purification

Qualities: Purification, communication, self-expression, speaking your truth, accepting your originality, expressing your authenticity, listening to others

Location: Throat region near the spine, behind the throat pit; the cervical plexus

Organs/systems: Throat, vocal cords, neck, ears, mouth, teeth, tongue, gums and jaw; nervous system, respiratory system

Endocrine glands: Thyroid and parathyroid glands

Colour: Blue

Flower: 16 petals

Elements: Sound/Ether

Deities: Sadhashiva, Sakini

Mantra: HAM

Sense: Hearing

Sensory organ: Ears

Organ of activity: Vocal cords

Animal: White elephant

Food: Blueberries, blackberries, blue grapes, blue currants, apples, herbal teas such as chamomile, elderberry, lemon and honey

Musical note: G

Crystals: Blue-lace agate, blue kyanite, turquoise, aquamarine, amazonite, angelate, apatite, blue calcite, lapis lazuli, larimar

Essential oils: Frankincense, chamomile, jasmine, cypress, lavender

Affirmation: "I am expressive"

Vishuddha is your communication centre. It helps you speak your truth and communicate with clarity and integrity. This chakra is responsible for transforming thoughts into sound through verbal communication. It is an expressive form of our soul, and is the reason why our voice can be very powerful: it can be used for comforting and uplifting others, or as a destructive weapon by pronouncing false accusations and lies.

The name Vishuddha means "purification" or "purified", according to yogic teaching. Purification occurs not only on the physical level, but also on the emotional and mental levels. For example, all the problems, traumatic past events and experiences that we have "swallowed" and suppressed during our lives are stored in our subconscious mind. When we leave emotional issues unfinished for long time, they still exist in a form of low-vibrational or negative energies within our subtle body, causing unbalance and blockages within our chakra system and manifesting in the physical body as pain or illness. It is said that Vishuddha is also directly linked to Manipura, as they are both a representation of the self.

This chakra is symbolized by a violet lotus with 16 petals. In the centre of the lotus is a white circle, the *yantra* of the element Ether. The *bija* mantra is HAM. The animal related to Vishuddha is a white elephant. As the energy centre of communication and expression, Vishuddha governs the ears, vocal cord, larynx, thyroid and parathyroid glands. This is the centre of vibration and sound, and through this chakra we can express what lies in our hearts, as well give our word on something. Lord Shiva is the controller of this chakra, and wind is the source of its energy.

Vishuddha is connected to Bindu Visarga (a chakra located at the back of the head, see page 160) and is known as the nectar and poison centre. The nectar drips down from Bindu to the back of the throat, where it splits in two: into a pure form and poison. The poison is discarded and the nectar (*amrit*) nourishes the body, ensuring good health and longevity. By practising different *mudras* and yoga techniques, you can purify the nectar in Vishuddha and release it, whereupon it becomes the nectar of immortality and the secret of youth. This process lies in the awakening of Vishuddha.

When meditating on Vishuddha, the mind becomes clear and light like Akasha (see page 78). Between the Vishuddha and Bindu chakras there is another smaller chakra, known as Lalana or Talumula (located at the back of the inner nasal cavity, above and beyond the palate), which works as a container where the amrit/nectar is stored. Khechari mudra is the action of rolling the tongue backward, so the tip of the tongue stimulates the Lalana chakra and the nectar can be released and purified in Vishuddha.

This chakra is also responsible for receiving thoughts and vibrations from other people. It enables you to tune into the thoughts and feelings of others, regardless of whether they are close or far away. These vibration waves or emotions are also received by Manipura chakra, although Vishuddha is the actual reception centre of thought waves and transmissions.

Different States of Vishuddha

Blocked Vishuddha

If Vishuddha is blocked, we may have issues expressing ourselves, communicating clearly with other people, and there might be a lot of arguing and misunderstanding. Maybe there are many secrets or a holding back of words. This chakra is connected to our listening ability, so if we are not behaving like a good listener, this is also a sign of a blocked Vishuddha. On a physical level a blocked Vishuddha manifests as a sore throat, dental issues, mouth ulcers, thyroid problems, neck pain, issues with hearing, jaw pain, shoulder pain, headaches and laryngitis.

Open Vishuddha

We have clear communication, no issues getting our words across, feel confident and have great creative expression. We are leaders, speak our truth and have the ability to listen to others. The sense of hearing becomes very sharp, but through the mind and not the ears.

Overactive Vishuddha

We are overly talkative, unable to listen, verbally abusive, highly critical, loud, very opinionated, gossipy, talk over others and use harsh words. We are basically using the gift of communication for negative energies.

Underactive Vishuddha

This is represented when we are introverted, shy, have difficulty speaking the truth, are unable to self-express, feel insecurity, hold back on expressing our needs and can't find our inner voice. We are afraid to talk, allowing others to dominate us verbally, and struggle to find our words. An underactive Vishuddha causes blockages within this chakra and the subtle system, as there is not enough flow of energy and it is not functioning at its optimal level. A great way to unblock it is through sound, because sound is an expressive form of our soul.

Modern Times and Vishuddha

How can we relate this chakra to modern times, and to our daily lives? Think about how many times you have wanted to say something to someone, but something has stopped you from saying it. Have you experienced that? How many times a day do you want to express your thoughts, opinions and feelings, but instead of doing this and getting them out, you choose to repress them instead. This situation is, unfortunately, part of our daily lives, and not saying or expressing whatever lies inside us is usually driven by fear.

Our emotions, ideas and opinions are all a form of energy that, once we repress it in our bodies, will create blockages in Vishuddha, and these blockages will eventually create imbalances in our entire system that may manifest as disease in our physical bodies. And all this because we didn't say what we wanted to say, or express our feelings toward someone or something. We are so used to repressing this, and ignoring things that we see – which in the first instance may be the right thing to do – that we are ignoring the fact that over time this will build up to a point where it can become unbearable, affecting us emotionally, physically and mentally.

I used to think that if I got a pound or a dollar every time I repressed my feelings and opinions, I would probably be rich by now – and you may have thought the same thing. But we need to explore this issue deeper and establish why we find it so hard sometimes to express ourselves and, most importantly, to speak our truth? If you have already read the sections on Muladhara, Svadhisthana and Manipura in modern times, this might resonate with you and you will be able to better understand this point.

Fear and ego are two main reasons why we hold back from expressing ourselves and speaking our minds. I have mentioned before that when one chakra is off-balance, it will impact on the others, and this is a good example of this situation. Fear is mainly a shadow aspect of Muladhara, and ego is the shadow side of Manipura, and these negative aspects are directly affecting Vishuddha. When we do energy work or energy healing, we must look further and deeper into the root cause of the problem. An experienced energy healer or Reiki practitioner will be able to determine where the problem has originated and give you the right guidance and treatment. So when we experience blockages in a particular chakra, there may be other chakras involved, too.

Vishuddha is all about speaking our truth and communicating with clarity and integrity. If our thoughts are originating from a place of love and light, then we will express that in words, whereas if our thoughts are coming from a place of fear, competition and ego, we will express just that and will also hear that.

This chakra is a great creator; it's our tool to communicate and express our authentic self, and anything that isn't in alignment with it will block this energy centre. Vishuddha gets blocked quite easily, as we are constantly speaking, communicating and listening throughout the day, although this chakra is also very easy to unblock. The best way to unblock and cleanse this chakra is through sound: the bija mantra HAM, an "Mmm" sound, Ujjayi breathing and yoga poses such as Matsyasana (Fish Pose). Ujjayi breathing, or "ocean breathing", is a technique often used in yoga practices. It consists of breathing in and out through your nose while creating a sound in your throat similar to the ocean.

When you find it difficult to express your emotions and your needs and to communicate clearly, I suggest that you look into the root cause of this issue. Self-confidence and self-worth could be two of the reasons, and these originate in Manipura. And fear of rejection and insecurities generally originate at Muladhara, Manipura, Anahata and Vishuddha. Insecurities block the flow of our life energy in the chakras, so it's always important to take some time to reflect on our feelings and try to understand where they originated from. When we understand ourselves and our energy patterns better, as well as the shadow side and our limiting self-beliefs, then we are open to go deeper in our healing journey and real healing can take place: on a soul level and on a cellular level.

I want you to stop for a moment and think of a time when you told someone, "I love you." Picture it in your mind, remember that moment and how you felt. Now I'm going to ask: did you give instructions to your brain to say "I love you" to that person, or did it seem like a nice feeling and the words "I love you" simply came out effortlessly from your mouth, like magic? With this exercise I want you to understand that whatever you feel or think will come out of our mouth naturally, just like the words "I love you."

Things that can help you to work with Vishuddha's energy are the following: no one is perfect; we all have past small or big traumas; and we are all carrying stuff with us that sometimes doesn't even belong to us, but it is for us to liberate ourselves from it in this lifetime. Not communicating properly will only make things worse. You see, once you start working and healing with the chakras, you will become more aware of yourself, of your thoughts and emotions; you are awake, you are mindful of yourself and of everything and everyone around you, and you will begin to operate more from your conscious mind, rather than being an emotional individual simply trying to survive in this world.

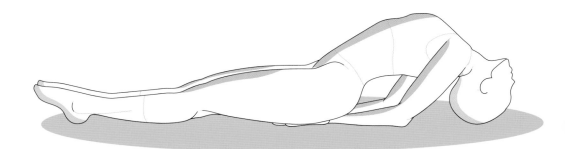

Healing Vishuddha

The idea of healing your chakras is to bring each chakra alive. It's about embodying and harnessing the energies and bringing them into your life, and using the energy of the chakras to help you live a better life.

Here are ten statements regarding Vishuddha's qualities. Use them as a self-assessment to help you determine how balanced or unbalanced your Vishuddha chakra is at this time. Each statements scores from 1 to 5, with 1 being "I strongly disagree" and 5 "I strongly agree". If you score 10, you have a balanced Vishuddha chakra: congratulations! If you score over 10 you are showing symptoms of an unbalanced chakra. The higher the score, the more blocked your Vishuddha is. Incorporating Vishuddha healing exercises and using the knowledge in this book can help you release the blockages that are present in this chakra and therefore increase the flow of *prana* in this energy centre.

1. I have difficulty speaking my truth
2. I have problems expressing my feelings
3. I'd rather talk than listen to others
4. I have problems trying to communicate clearly and be understood
5. I feel like most of the time I haven't been heard
6. I suffer regularly from throat problems
7. I am not the type of person who feels comfortable standing by others, when necessary
8. I am constantly arguing with others to get my point across
9. I usually find myself holding back what I want to say
10. I have neck/cervical problems

Vishuddha healing is the practice of stimulating, awakening, opening, cleansing and strengthening this chakra. To heal Vishuddha, focus on doing the exercises, tips and healing techniques described here for at least three or four continuous days. Use the food, crystals, sound, colours, positive affirmations, meditation and yoga mentioned – basically everything that is related to this chakra – to cleanse and strengthen this energy centre.

By working on this chakra you can create spaciousness around the throat and neck, through which profound spiritual truths can flow. One of the best and easiest ways to tap into this chakra is by chanting HAM or humming "Mmm". The chanting has to be loud enough that you are able to hear yourself and feel the vibrations in your body, specifically around the mouth and throat. Remember: try to speak your truth as much as possible.

Yoga Poses for Vishuddha

Yoga poses that move the neck into extension and flexion can open and activate this chakra. They are also very beneficial on a physical level to treat thyroid problems.

- Bitilasana Marjaryasana and Simhasana (Cat/Cow with Lion's Breath)
- Sarvangasana (Shoulderstand)
- Matsyasana (Fish Pose)
- Chakrasana (Wheel Pose)
- Head rolls and neck stretches
- Astangasana (Eight Limbs Pose)

Nourishment for Vishuddha

Eat all the blue foods that are available to you, including blueberries and blackberries. You can also have coconut water, raw honey, plums, herbal teas and fruits that grow on trees, such as apples, pears, oranges and apricots. Nourish your body by eating citrus fruit. Take hot drinks, soups and a light diet that is vegan and plant-based.

Meditation

1. Sit in a cross-legged position or on a chair. Close your eyes, then bring your awareness to Vishuddha chakra.

2. Breathe into Vishuddha, visualizing expansion of the colour blue as you inhale and exhale.

3. You can apply essential oils on your pulse points, play music for Vishuddha or do this meditation chanting the *bija* mantra HAM. Repeat some positive affirmations for this chakra (see page 289).

Mudra for Vishuddha: Vishuddha *Mudra*

Duration: 5 minutes

1. Sitting with crossed legs, interlock your fingers, with the palms facing up.

2. Join the tip of the thumbs. Meditate on this *mudra* for a while.

Vishuddha Zen Moments

Ensure that you are communicating with dignity all the time. If you are finding it difficult to express yourself, try writing down what you want to say and reading it out loud; listen to yourself saying those words, but remember that it is important you feel that you have been heard and understood. Whatever you choose to do, try to achieve some Zen moments that are guided by intuition rather than by conscious effort.

Here are some suggestions to help you reconnect with Vishuddha:
- Wear the colour blue
- Sing
- Chant
- Gargle with warm lemon water
- Recite poems
- Listen to healing music
- Dance to your favourite song
- Practise active listening

"Today I only speak the truth. My ears only hear the truth. My entire being only expresses the truth."

Sixth Chakra: Ajna or Third Eye Chakra

AJNA ASSOCIATIONS
Name: Ajna = command
Qualities: Vision, intellect, comprehension, intuition, connection, perception of subtle dimensions, imagination, psychic abilities related to clairvoyance and clairaudience, connection to wisdom, insight, decision-making, spiritual awareness
Location: At the centre between the eyebrows, at the very top of the spinal cord; the pineal gland
Organs/systems: Eyes, brain
Endocrine glands: Pineal and pituitary glands
Colour: Indigo
Flower: Two petals
Elements: Light/Ether, beyond the five elements
Deities: Paramshiva and Hakini
Mantra: OM
Sense: Sight/perception
Sensory organ: The mind
Organ of activity: The mind
Animal: None
Food: Blackberries, blackcurrants, plums, purple grapes, raisins, elderberries, blueberries, figs, aubergines, purple asparagus, purple cabbage, purple peppers
Musical note: A
Crystals: Amethyst, azurite, clear quartz, sodalite, labradorite, blue aventurine
Essential oils: Palo santo, vetiver, frankincense, cypress, laurel, sandalwood, ylang-ylang, lavender, clary sage
Affirmation: "I see"

The word Ajna comes from the Sanskrit root meaning "to know" or "to obey"; literally, it means "command". Ajna is known as the "Guru chakra" because it is here that the directions of the inner gurus are heard in the deepest state of meditation. This might be why this chakra usually seems to be the favourite when people start learning about the chakras and spirituality, because everyone gets excited about the possibility of developing their physic powers, connecting with the higher realms and having a third-eye opening or awakening. In Hindu tradition, Ajna signifies the ability to see the spiritual world and is believed to reveal insights about the future. Ajna is the chakra of the mind that represents a higher level of awareness.

It is located in our forehead in between the eyes. With our two physical eyes we see the material world, and with our "third eye" we are able to see the spiritual world: it forms the boundary between human and divine consciousness. This chakra also transcends time, and enables us to see both the inner and outer worlds. Ajana harmonizes the two hemispheres of the brain. Regular meditation with visualization is highly recommended to support the energy of this chakra, so that we can manifest our desires in the physical world. It is said that Ajna is linked to our arms and hands, because what we see with our third eye we can manifest and create with our hands.

This chakra can lead you to higher level of consciousness, and to a realization of wholeness and oneness. It can access clairvoyant abilities, because we can see the future with our third eye. In deeper states of meditation the practitioner receives commands and guidance from the guru, and from the divine or Higher Self, via this chakra. Ajna is the point where the two nadis Ida and Pingala merge with Sushumna. When this happens, a transformation of the individual's consciousness takes place. This union of the three nadis is achieved through regular meditation, pranayama and asana practices that bring balance between the energies in our body and eventually awakening of Kundalini.

Ajna is represented by a lotus with two petals, which symbolize the Sun and the Moon, or the Pingala nadi right-side positive force and the Ida nadi left-side negative force. The Ida and Pingala nadis are responsible for the experience of duality and converge at this point with Sushumna nadi, carrying the spiritual force. Ajna is also associated with the pineal gland. This gland usually stops developing and growing as we get older, and this is why not everyone develops physic abilities, even though we have the capacity to do so. Ajna is known as the "eye of knowledge" because it is the channel through which the spiritual aspirant receives guidance and revelations.

To reach Ajna requires dedication, discipline and a firm belief. In the physical world this is the final chakra. Ajna activation means achieving higher levels of consciousness that can open the door to the activation of Sahasrara chakra.

This is the coolest chakra in our system – at least that's how I see it. Just thinking about the fact that we have a third eye through which we can see beyond any physical form and have psychic powers is cool. The physical body and the subtle body never cease to amaze me. We are indeed incredible creatures and must honour and embody that. A great way to start tapping into this energy is by bringing your thoughts, ideas, projects and dreams into your third eye – by this, I mean picturing them clearly in front of you, like a movie, and almost living and feeling them. It is more powerful to act as if you have already got that job, can see what you are doing on your first day, how your first week is going to develop, what will you be wearing, who will you be talking to and even having lunch with at your new office, rather than sitting in your living room saying, "I hope I get that job." Do you get me? The power of thought and visualization.

It is also important to clarify that the pineal gland and Ajna are the same thing, and Ajna is also connected to the pituitary gland, which is Sahasrara. The pineal gland acts as a lock on the pituitary gland. When the pineal gland is healthy, the pituitary gland's functions are controlled. However, the pineal gland starts to degenerate between the ages of eight and ten, so the pituitary gland begins secreting hormones that instigate our sexual consciousness, sensuality and the way we present ourselves in the world, and then we start losing our connection with our spiritual heritage. By practising different yoga and Tantra techniques it is possible to maintain a healthy pineal gland.

Different States of Ajna

Blocked Ajna

A blocked Ajna manifests in our physical body as headaches, migraines, problems with vision, dizziness, insomnia, mental confusion and stress.

Open Ajna

If we experience visions beyond the physical realm, then we might be in tune with our intuition and able to perceive when environments or people don't feel right. We are able to manifest, have psychic abilities and a good connection with the Spirit world. We are also able to make decisions.

Overactive Ajna

This means that we are unable to focus and there's a lack of good judgement; we might experience hallucinations and disassociation from the physical world, excessive dreaming, stress, mental fog and anxiety.

Underactive Ajna

We are closed to new ideas, disconnected from our inner voice or wisdom, anxious, clinging to the past, unable to see the big picture and feel a lack of focus and purpose, confusion and depression.

Modern Times and Ajna

Ajna represents your connection to wisdom and insight. It is your sixth sense that enables you to access your inner guidance – the guidance that comes from deep within you.

One of the main characteristics of an off-balance Ajna chakra is the inability to see the bigger picture, and difficulty in making decisions. If only we were more connected to our inner guidance, we would be able to make better decisions in our lives, saving us a lot of pain and suffering, right? We would be able to choose better leaders for our nations, better jobs, better partners, and so on. To access this inner wisdom and tap into our psychic powers, we must listen carefully and pay attention to the guidance signs, and to the whispering voice that most of the time we ignore or don't trust.

To access this centre and enjoy the benefits of Ajna we only need to train it and use it. It's that simple. What we find challenging is sitting in stillness in order to achieve this. Tapping into the energy of the third eye is very simple because it is already within us, but to open this chakra requires dedication and discipline.

You can use Ajna to tap into your intuition, but also to create the life you want, and you can manifest your deepest desires through this chakra. Where you focus your awareness plays a key role in what you are creating in your life. What most people do these days is focus on the negative – on what is lacking in their lives – homing in what they don't want or like. In this way they are simply driving their attention to these negative aspects of their lives, without realizing that they are energetically drawing more of this energy toward them. It is important to stay positive and to focus on your highest intentions.

Your thoughts, emotions, beliefs, attitudes, words and actions create your reality: your life experience. This is why we need a third eye to help us see beyond what lies in front of us. Ajna give us vision, and drops the false illusions that lie in front of our eyes.

This chakra can be strengthened with regular meditation because you are working with a visual chakra. One of my favourite ways to manifest things is by daydreaming. Try to see yourself enjoying that holiday, getting that job or driving that new car, almost as if you are watching a movie. Turn your attention to your intentions and you will see how much of a creator you are.

We hear a lot people complaining about how cruel this world is, how hard life is, and so on. But I wonder what would happen if the majority of people cultivated the habit of turning such statements into something more positive, so that instead of feeling sorry and powerless, we trust our inner guidance and inner power to manifest and create a beautiful world. If we see ourselves as beings able to change our life experience through our intentions and our positive thoughts, then I'm sure it would be a much better world, full of abundance and opportunities for everyone.

One interesting note: Ajna is more active in females than it is in males. Women are more sensitive and psychic than men, and this why you have probably heard that women have a sixth sense… because it is true. However, in most people this inner ability remains dormant. Unless this chakra is awakened, we won't be able to gain knowledge and understanding and see beyond the world's reality. We will remain "blind" to the real possibilities and potential of the world!

To reach Ajna chakra requires dedicated practice, discipline, effort and patience. With our current level of consciousness, we are just not in the state of mind to reach Sahasrara. However, once Ajna is active, we develop psychic abilities and develop a superior perception on how to attain Sahasrara.

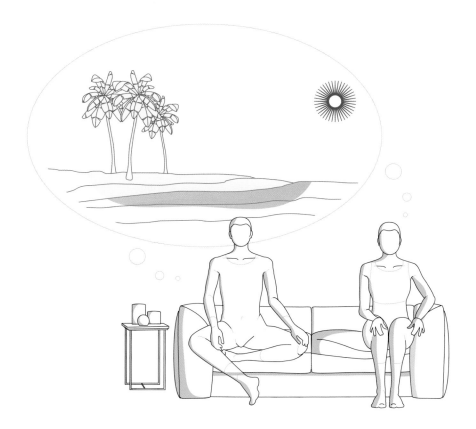

Healing Ajna

The idea of healing your chakras is to bring each chakra alive. It's about embodying and harnessing the energies and bringing them into your life, and using the energy of the chakras to help you live a better life.

Here are ten statements regarding Ajna's qualities. Use them as a self-assessment to help you determine how balanced or unbalanced your Ajna chakra is at this time. Each statements scores from 1 to 5, with 1 being "I strongly disagree" and 5 "I strongly agree". If you score 10, you have a balanced Ajna chakra: congratulations! If you score over 10 you are showing symptoms of an unbalanced chakra. The higher the score, the more blocked your Ajna is. Incorporating Ajna healing exercises and using the knowledge in this book can help you release the blockages that are present in this chakra and therefore increase the flow of *prana* in this energy centre.

1. I find difficult to connect with my intuition
2. It's hard for me to develop psychic abilities
3. I don't feel a connection with the spirit world
4. I have constants headaches and migraines
5. I have blurry vision
6. I feel stressed and mentally foggy
7. I usually have problems visualizing what I want to manifest
8. I dream excessively
9. I sometimes feel disassociated from this world
10. I find it hard to open my mind to new ideas

Ajna healing is the practice of stimulating, awakening, opening, cleansing and strengthening this chakra. To heal Ajna, focus on doing the exercises, tips and healing techniques described here for at least three or four continuous days. Use the food, crystals, sound, colours, positive affirmations, meditation and yoga mentioned – basically everything that is related to this chakra – to cleanse and strengthen this energy centre.

Working on this chakra requires *sadhana* (consistent spiritual practice), a lot of meditation and physical practice, such as yoga *asanas*. Tap into your intuition by asking your inner guidance to give you the answers to a certain situation: ask for revelations and messages in your dreams; try to guess what will happen in your day or who will you bump into – these are fun ways to start tapping into the energy of Ajna. From time to time give a little massage to your third eye with essential oils. By opening and building awareness in this chakra, you will begin to see everything in your life more clearly and can start to see things as they are, without the influence of ego. It is so important to work on healing Ajna, because a severe blockage of energy in this chakra can lead to mental confusion and a poor ability to make decisions and learn new things, trouble sleeping, and so on.

I love placing a crystal on my third eye and lying down for 20 minutes, while visualizing a new project or holiday.

Yoga Poses for Ajna

Add these postures to your yoga practice, or even as part of your exercise routine.

- Balasana (Child's Pose)
- Trataka (candle-gazing)
- Adho Mukha Svanasana (Downward-facing Dog)
- Ardha Pincha Mayurasana (Dolphin Pose)
- Uttanasana (Forward Fold)
- Chaturanga Dandasana (Four-limbed Staff Pose)
- Vajrasana (Thunderbolt Pose)
- Makarasana (Crocodile Pose)
- Utkatasana (Chair Pose)
- Bhramari *pranayama* (Humming-bee Breath)

Nourishment for Ajna

Enjoy omega-3-rich foods, such as nuts and seeds (walnuts, flaxseeds and chia seeds), as well as indigo foods like blueberries, raspberries, blackberries, purple kale, aubergines, purple cabbage, purple sweet potatoes and cacao. Take plant oils such as flaxseed oil, soybean oil and canola oil, and haricot beans. Some texts about chakras recommend eating omega-3-rich fish such as salmon and sardines, but I leave it up the reader whether or not to consume animal products.

Meditation

1. Sit in a cross-legged position or on a chair. Close your eyes, then bring your awareness
   to Ajna chakra.

2. Breathe into this chakra, visualizing expansion of the colour indigo as you inhale and exhale.

3. You can apply essential oils on your pulse points, play music for Ajna or do this meditation
   chanting the *bija* mantra OM. Repeat some positive affirmations for this chakra (see page 290).

Try to start meditating more. Tap on the energy of this chakra and connect with it,
so that you become best pals. Once you start getting more in tune with Anja,
things start flowing and you will see things, people and situations with clarity
– the veils will fall away. You will have more control of your life and this can be
something really powerful, especially during difficult times.

Mudra for Ajna: Kalesvara *Mudra*

1. Sitting comfortably with crossed legs, curl your fingers together, except the middle fingers.

2. Bring your thumbs together, then let all the fingers touch each other.

3. You can place this *mudra* on your forehead while chanting OM. Alternatively do this *mudra*
   while meditating.

Ajna Zen Moments

This is a very mystical chakra. Don't be afraid to follow your intuition and to trust it. You need to work with it so that you know when it is your inner guidance communicating with you, and not your mind. Aim to achieve Zen moments that are guided by intuition rather than by conscious effort.

Here are some suggestions to help you reconnect with Ajna:

- Wear the colour indigo
- Sit outside with your third eye facing the sunlight
- Daydream
- Do a *yantra* meditation (see page 227)
- Do some colouring
- Massage Ajna (the forehead) gently
- Do an OM meditation
- Practise *Nadi Shodhana pranayama* (see page 272)

"Every time I close my eyes and imagine my dream life I am a step closer to that dream."

Seventh Chakra: Sahasrara or Crown Chakra

SAHASRARA ASSOCIATIONS
Name: *Sahasrara* = thousand-petalled
Qualities: Wisdom, awareness, intelligence, unity, connection, bliss, awareness of the Higher Self, consciousness, sacredness
Location: The top centre of the head
Organs/systems: Head, brain, ears, eyes; skeletal and muscular systems, nervous system
Endocrine glands: Pineal gland, hypothalamus, pituitary glands
Colour: White or violet
Flower: 1,000 petals
Element: Spirit
Deity: Shiva
Mantra: OM or silence
Sense: None
Sensory organ: None
Organ of activity: None
Animal: None
Food: This chakra is linked to spiritual nourishment rather than physical nourishment; a clean, natural, high-quality, organic fruit-and-vegetable diet should be maintained
Musical note: B
Crystals: Clear quartz crystal, moonstone, amethyst, lepidolite, selenite, clear calcite, magnesite, celestite
Essential oils: Rosewood, cedarwood, sandalwood, frankincense, lavender, palo santo
Affirmation: "I am divine"

Sahasrara is the golden portal that allows the influx of cosmic energy into our beings. It is not really a chakra as such, or one of the physical chakras, but many people call it the seventh chakra. It is located just above of the top of the head and is known as the "Hole of Brahman", and as the dwelling house of the human soul. Sahasrara is the chakra that connects you with the spiritual realm and your Higher Self. It is associated with bliss, oneness, beliefs, understanding, connection, Spirit and higher consciousness. Sahasrara is the biggest energy centre of the seven main chakras, as it is the one that receives all the energy from the universe and distributes it to the rest of the chakras. When you have overcome and balanced all six previous chakras, you can transcend Sahasrara into the higher realms. This chakra is very light in comparison with the other chakras. It radiates gold and silver light that represents the divine and the Higher Self "I am".

Sahasrara is mostly concerned with unity and separation issues. This is our root with our father – not just our Earthly father, but our Heavenly Father too. If there is tension in the head, that means there is some form of tension in a specific part of the conscious mind. The person may feel as if they are hiding from everyone and not seeing what is truly in their soul. This is the hardest part to clarify: accepting the truth about your situation can be mind-numbing until the mind can take time to meditate on the issue and finally accept it. The counterbalance here is that if we continue to do something that makes us unhappy, it can lead to our health becoming worse.

The word Sahasrara means "thousand-petalled", and for this reason this chakra is represented by a lotus with 1,000 petals; this implies Sahasrara's magnitude and its significance are vast. Sahasrara is the totality – it transcends all concepts. Sahasrara is the culmination of yoga. When Kundalini shakti rises up and reaches Sahasrara, that is known as the union between Lord Shiva and Shakti. Shiva and Shakti merging together represents the union of the ultimate consciousness with prana, and this is the moment of self-realization. The union of these two forces is the beginning of a great experience and the death of man: not necessarily a physical death, but the death of mundane awareness or individual awareness. There is only one single awareness, one experience. This experience is known as Samadhi – the pure purpose of yoga – and by opening and awakening the six previous chakras, Kundalini can rise up all the way up from Muladhara chakra through the Sushumna nadi to Sahasrara.

Different States of Sahasrara

Blocked Sahasrara

If Sahasrara is blocked, we may have feelings of loneliness, depression, ungroundedness, a lack of connection with the Source and with people, with the universe, and no understanding of the reason for our existence. In the physical body we might feel a bit foggy, have learning difficulties, pressure in the head, headaches or a sensation of heaviness on the top of the head.

Open Sahasrara

We feel a real connection with the Source. We experience universal love and completeness, feel wise and aware of our spirituality and our purpose in the world. We are our true selves, full of vitality and divine energy. We feel balanced and connected to the higher dimensions.

Overactive Sahasrara

We might have dogmatic ideas, be very judgemental and feel ungrounded or have an addiction to spirituality. There may be a disconnection from the physical world and a neglect of physical needs. Lack of direction, feeling lost, mental confusion and an over-imaginative disassociation from the body may also occur.

Underactive Sahasrara

We may feel disconnected from the Higher Self and the highest consciousness, confusion, uncertainty, lack of inspiration, with low energy and vitality, a lack of awareness in our lives, spiritual ignorance, limiting beliefs, depression, suicidal thoughts, a lack of purpose or spiritual connection, fear and exhaustion.

Modern Times and Sahasrara

During my training as yoga teacher, I learned that we were born enlightened; that we came into this world with all our chakras open and holding a *dharma*, or true life purpose. It then became a matter of time before all truth and awareness got lost deep within our consciousness, cluttered by our surroundings and the dogma that we are fed from the day we are born.

We came into this world enlightened and will leave this world enlightened – how many lifetimes it will take us to get there is another story. Sahasrara helps us to get there by assisting us in connecting with the divine and our true purpose. This chakra is the centre that connects us to the cosmic universal energy and our Higher Self. The more our Sahasrara is open and healthy, the more we will receive this high energy into our being.

This is why most people who are not connected to their souls and their spirituality find it difficult to know what their purpose in life is. They haven't got that connection yet; they haven't received the higher energies that will help them remember who they truly are and why they are here.

Sahasrara is a high-consciousness portal to the spiritual world and higher dimensions. If the gate is open, we will be connecting with an infinite celestial guidance that we will use to navigate through our lives with purpose. Connecting to Sahasrara means living a life of happiness, good health and purpose. We are able to connect with our soul, with the Source and with others.

This is the last chakra that connects to our physical body.

Healing Sahasrara

The idea of healing your chakras is to bring each chakra alive. It's about embodying and harnessing the energies and bringing them into your life, and using the energy of the chakras to help you live a better life.

Here are ten statements regarding Sahasrara's qualities. Use them as a self-assessment to help you determine how balanced or unbalanced your Sahasrara chakra is at this time. Each statements scores from 1 to 5, with 1 being "I strongly disagree" and 5 "I strongly agree". If you score 10, you have a balanced Sahasrara chakra: congratulations! If you score over 10 you are showing symptoms of an unbalanced chakra. The higher the score, the more blocked your Sahasrara is. Incorporating Sahasrara healing exercises and using the knowledge in this book can help you release the blockages that are present in this chakra and therefore increase the flow of *prana* in this energy centre.

1. I am a very judgemental person
2. I find it hard to connect well with others
3. I usually don't feel supported and guided by a supreme force in the universe
4. I have little interest in, and curiosity about, spirituality
5. I don't regularly have vivid dreams
6. I don't see myself as part of the divine
7. I have little connection with the Higher Self
8. I find it hard to understand oneness in spirituality
9. I easily have mental confusion
10. I have difficulty understanding my purpose in life

Sahasrara healing is the practice of stimulating, awakening, opening, cleansing and strengthening this chakra. To heal Sahasrara, focus on doing the exercises, tips and healing techniques described here for at least three or four continuous days. Use the food, crystals, sound, colours, positive affirmations, meditation and yoga mentioned – basically everything that is related to this chakra – to cleanse and strengthen this energy centre.

This chakra is the highest point of awareness. It gives us access to higher states of consciousness, as we open to what lies beyond our physical reality and physical experiences. All six previous chakras are merged here. Everything becomes one, and all of the chakras, their colours and their elements are connected in Sahasrara.

To reach Sahasrara, physical and mental cleansing must have taken place, and this is all about divinity, purity and the supreme. I find that the best way to connect with this chakra is through a regular meditation practice and by embarking on the yoga path. Sahasrara represents the end of yoga.

Yoga Poses for Sahasrara

Practise physical activities like running or yoga to embrace who you are.

- Ardha Chadrasana (Half Moon Pose)
- Virabhadrasana (Warrior 1)
- Sirsasana (Headstand)
- Savasana (Corpse Pose)
- Ardha Padmasana (Half Lotus Pose)
- Vrikshasana (Tree Pose)
- Inversion poses
- Restorative yoga poses
- Paschimottanasasa (Seated Forward Bend)

Nourishment for Sahasrara

This chakra is more about detoxing or fasting than it is about eating. However, those lacking in Sahasrara can benefit from fresh, organic, whole and nourishing food. Drink herbal teas instead of coffee; avoid caffeine, alcohol, recreational drugs and sugar.

Meditation

Duration: 5 minutes, or as long as you wish

1. Sit in a cross-legged position or on a chair. Close your eyes, then bring
   your awareness to Sahasrara.

2. Breathe into Sahasrara, visualizing expansion of the colour white/silver as
   you inhale and exhale.

3. You can apply essential oils on your pulse points, play music for Sahasrara
   or do this meditation chanting the *bija* mantra OM. Repeat some positive
   affirmations for this chakra (see page 291).

Mudra for Sahasrara: Hakini *Mudra*

Duration: a few minutes

1. Sitting comfortably with crossed legs, join all the fingertips together:
   thumb with thumb, index finger with index finger, and so on.

2. Keep the hands open, making a round shape. Meditate on this *mudra* for
   a while.

Sahasrara Zen Moments

Go outdoors, breathe fresh air, feel the breeze and sunshine touching every cell in your being. Establish meaningful connections in life. Surround yourself with your soul family. Nourish not only your physical body, but your soul, too. Detox yourself from negative people, environments and thoughts. Practise spiritual activities, such as rituals and prayers. Whatever you choose to do, try to achieve some Zen moments that are guided by intuition rather than by conscious effort.

Here are some suggestions to help you reconnect with Sahasrara:

- Do some journaling
- Spend time in nature
- Rest
- Do nourishing activities
- Help others
- Do charity work
- Connect with your spirituality
- Pray
- Raise your vibration

"I am connected to the divine. I am supported and guided by the higher dimensions and spiritual realms in the universe and beyond."

Bindu Visarga Chakra

We know very little about the Bindu chakra, which is considered the source of creation, because it goes beyond the realm of all experience – even in Tantric texts there is not much about it. Bindu Visarga means "falling on the drop", and this chakra represents the manifestation of creation and consciousness. It is situated beneath the whorl of hair at the tip of the head, and is where Indian holy men (called Brahmin) grow a tuft of hair to honour this chakra. The Bindu chakra is considered the point at which creation begins and may become unity. This point lies below Sahasrara and above Ajna.

Bindu is represented by a lotus flower with 23 petals, with a crescent moon and a white drop, which is the nectar dripping down to Vishuddha chakra. This chakra is said to be the source of bindu fluid, which contains the divine nectar called amrit, the mystical elixir of immortality. This sweet nectar drops down to Vishuddha, where it is purified for further use in the body. As mentioned earlier (see page 127), Bindu Visarga and Vishuddha are interconnected via the network of veins that passes the interior part of the nasal cavity, passing through Lalana chakra, which sits at the top of the back of the palate. Therefore when Vishuddha gets stimulated and awakened, Bindu and Lalana are also activated.

Bindu Visarga is a centre for good health. It supports physical and mental recuperation, and promotes inner peace, clarity and balance. Meditating on this chakra can relieve anxiety and depression. It is said that when this chakra awakens, the sound OM is heard and one realizes the source of all creation.

Exercises for Bindu Visarga

Any type of yoga *asanas* that involve inversion are great for awakening this chakra.
You could try the following:

- Sirsasana (Headstand)
- Sarvangasana (Shoulderstand)
- Ardha Sarvangasana (Half Shoulderstand)
- Ujjayi *pranayama* (Ocean breathing)
- Khechari *mudra* (Rolling Tongue *mudra*)

Minor Chakras

By this point I believe you have already realized what incredible beings we are, inside and out. Just like our amazing human anatomy, our subtle body is beautiful, perfect and complex. We have 114 chakras and 72,000 *nadis*, and of those chakras, 112 lie within our physical body and two outside the human body. In addition to the seven main chakras that we have explored in this book, we have 21 minor chakras and 86 micro chakras.

Minor and micro chakras are equally important, and the fact that we don't hear much about them doesn't make them less significant. They help to regulate the flow of energy within our bodies. The minor chakras are small points that fuel the major chakras in the body. Good examples are Bindu Visarga (see page 160), Lalana chakra and the thymus chakra – they are very much related to the main chakra they are nearest to. Minor chakras are also known as the pressure points that are used in Traditional Chinese Medicine, such as reflexology or acupuncture.

In Indian tradition when you greet someone you say *Namaste*, and this greeting usually comes with a hand gesture that involves pressing the hands together in the Prayer Position in front of the chest. One of the reasons behind this, as explained to me by my guru, is activation of the chakras (or pressure points) in the hands. By doing this gesture, you will remember the other person's name, and it is also a more meaningful way to greet someone.

The minor chakras that we know about are:
- One under each collarbone, totalling two
- One in each palm of the hand, totalling two
- One on each sole of the foot, totalling two
- One above both eyes, between the nose and the eyebrow, totalling two
- One in every reproductive organ
- One in the liver
- One in the stomach
- Two in the spleen
- One at the back of the knees, totalling two
- One in the vagus nerve at the thymus gland
- One near Manipura

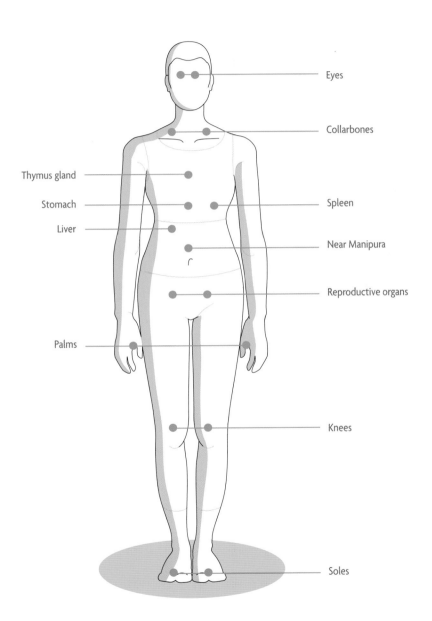

Eyes

Collarbones

Thymus gland

Stomach

Spleen

Liver

Near Manipura

Reproductive organs

Palms

Knees

Soles

Hand Chakras

These chakras are located in the palms of the hand and enable you to both give and receive energy. Some people believe that the left hand receives energy while the right hand sends energy out. Through your hands there is an exchange of energies when you shake hands with others, when you touch people and even when you hit someone. The hands – and therefore the chakras in the hands – are associated with Anahata and are seen as an extension of this centre. You should use your hands in a positive way to create beautiful things for yourself and others. With your hands you should serve the purposes of Sahasrara.

The hands are vehicles for us to express and interact with others. When these chakras are blocked, there are usually creativity blocks and difficulty in connecting with other people. The hand mudra of the Prayer Position reflects this connection. When we press both palms together we are activating these energy points and our bodies. From an energetic standpoint, hands are very sensitive and powerful, and are used to channel spiritual energy for healing by Reiki practitioners. Hands can also be used for scanning your aura for hotspots that need your attention. You can use your hands to heal others with techniques such as massage or reflexology.

Try using your hands to create artistic works, such as painting, pottery and drawing; and for caring for others. Massage your hands from time to time and practise gratitude toward them. Take a moment to observe the palms and backs of the hands. Know your hands well, and put nice intentions into them. Be grateful to your hands for serving you and others. Look after them, feel the touch of your hands, look at the size of them, see if you can see a mark that you didn't know was there. The more you practise gratitude by caring for your hands, the more abundance will come your way.

Last but not least, each of the five elements in our bodies is represented in each of the fingers, so we can actually regulate the flow of energy and balance the elements within us using hand mudras (see pages 234–237).

Knee Chakras

The knee chakras are located in the hollow part at the back of your knee joint. It is believed that these chakras are associated with fears that can influence our progress in life. (Do you remember which chakra is associated with fear, and which part of the body is associated with that chakra? Yes, that's right: I'm talking about Muladhara.) So by practising yoga, or simple joint movements in your knees, you are able to release some of the trapped energies present in that part of the body, to free the flow of *prana* and increase flexibility.

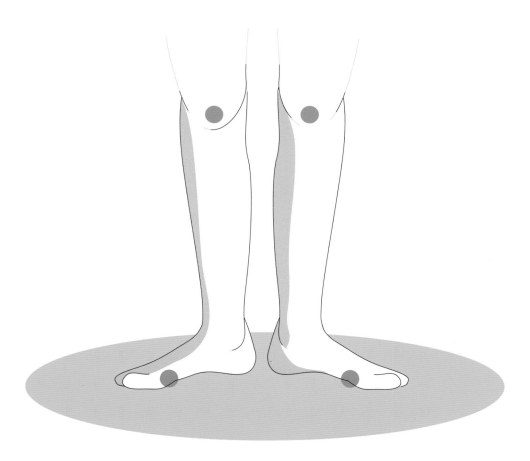

Soles of the Feet Chakras

These chakras are located in the centre of the arch of the foot. They are grounding and balancing chakras. Have you ever wondered why a yoga teacher asks you to press your whole feet on the mat, and to spread your toes, when doing a standing or balancing pose? It is because, by doing so, you are activating all these chakras on the soles of your feet and connecting energetically to the Earth's energy. These feet chakras are also connected to the body's major organs. If you have ever had a reflexology session, you will know how relaxing and healing it can feel; and an experienced reflexology practitioner can tell you what the problem in your organs is, simply by feeling your feet.

Practise regular foot massage, and soak your feet in warm water from time to time. Take care of your feet. Sometimes we don't pay much attention to our feet and we take them for granted. We forget that they not only help to take us from point A to point B, but also help us to move forward in life, feel grounded and connected to this Earth.

You can massage your feet with essential oils for grounding and balancing if you feel dizzy and disconnected from your body, or place a grounding crystal such as haematite or smoky quartz under your feet.

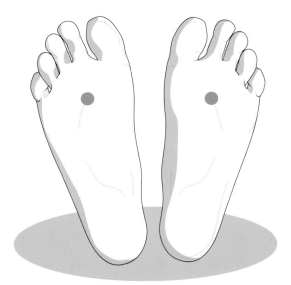

Earth Star Chakra

This chakra is also known as the Super Root Chakra, and is located about 30cm (12in) below your feet. The Earth Star connects you to the Earth's energy, which flows to Muladhara chakra. It is also the chakra that is responsible for making you feel grounded and connected to your body and to Mother Earth. This chakra can become blocked when we are too immersed in a city lifestyle: desk jobs, concrete buildings and surroundings, a lack of nature and sunlight.

A great way to reconnect with this chakra and dissolve any blockages is by going back to nature. Appreciate the colours, smells and living things that Mother Earth offers us. Try hugging a tree, or try grounding meditation, where you visualize roots coming out of the soles of your feet.

Whenever life gets tough, come back to nature. Nature is the best medicine for the mind, body and Spirit.

Lunar Chakra

The Lunar Chakra is an extension of the crown chakra, Sahasrara. It is located above Sahasrara. It is usually represented in colours such as silver and white. This is a very light and subtle chakra of a high-vibrational frequency. It is associated with the Moon and feminine energies. It is believed that this chakra connects us to our souls and true self, which is why this chakra is also known as the Soul Star Chakra.

You can consciously tap into the energy of this chakra by connecting to the Moon and its faces. Moon rituals are a great way to activate the Lunar Chakra. This is one of the most spiritual chakras that we know. It is a portal that connect us to higher realms and astral dimensions, opening us to the unknown, sacred and spiritual.

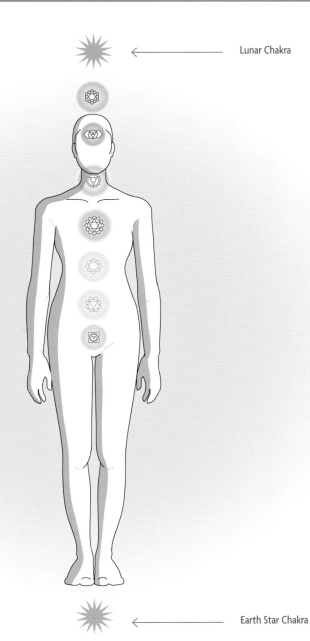

Lunar Chakra

Earth Star Chakra

4

ENERGY
HEALING

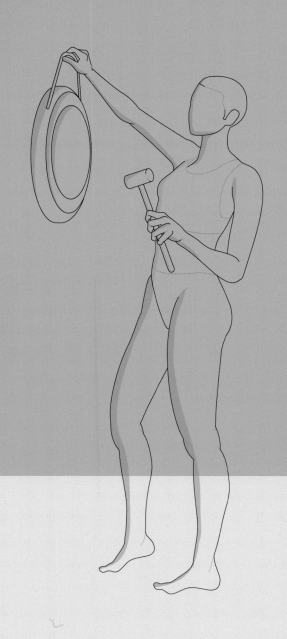

What Is Energy Healing?

We are energetic beings, and everything is energy. Scientists have proven this to be true. Each layer of the energy body has a different function and is associated with a different chakra, which together affect different areas of the physical body. The chakras and acupuncture points are openings for energy to flow into and out of the aura (energy body). This energy is associated with a form of consciousness, and thus we experience the exchange of energy in the forms of seeing, hearing, feeling, sensing, intuiting or direct knowing. It is important to open the chakras and increase our energy flow because the more energy we circulate, the healthier we are. Illness in the system is caused by an imbalance of energy or a blocking of the flow of energy. In other words, a lack of flow in the human energy system might eventually lead to illness and disease. It also distorts our perceptions, dampens our feelings and prevents us from living a joyful life.

So what causes an imbalance or block in the flow of energy? Today the majority of people have been conditioned to react to unpleasant experiences by blocking their feelings, which stops a great deal of their natural energy flow. As an example of this: if someone is rejected many times when she tries to show her love to another person, she eventually stops showing that love by trying to stop the inner feelings of love. In order to do this, she will have to stop the energy flow through Anahata. When the energy flow is stopped or slowed down, the development of Anahata is affected, which eventually means that a physical problem will probably result if the energy does not start to flow smoothly again.

The same process works for all the chakras. Whenever a person blocks the experiences he is having, he in turn blocks his chakras, which blocks the flow of universal life-force energy, which in turn causes blockages, disruptions, weaknesses or imbalances in the chakras. This can be caused by many different situations in our lives, such as: emotional or physical trauma, injury, negative self-talk, toxicity, nutritional depletion, a destructive lifestyle and relationships, neglect of self and lack of love for oneself or others, emotions that are not expressed in a healthy way, childhood traumas, cultural conditioning, a limited belief system, bad habits or even just a lack of attention. Difficulties abound in life for each one of us, and we develop a coping strategy. If these difficulties persist, our coping strategies become energetic patterns, anchored in the body and psyche as defence structures. It is important to recognize the blocks that we carry, to locate and understand their source and then heal them.

Energy healing is excellent for any physical, mental, emotional and spiritual issues. I recommend starting off with energy and aura-cleansing (see page 194). I also suggest regular energy-healing therapy such as Reiki (see page 178). Long-term practice of whole-body energy healing will restore the general condition of the body. It will open the energy channels, which will allow the body to deal properly and naturally with stress and the build-up of toxins, along with coping with anxiety and depression.

Some of the health benefits from receiving energy healing are:
- It creates deep relaxation and helps the body to release stress and tension
- It accelerates the body's self-healing abilities
- It aids better sleep
- It reduces blood pressure
- It can help with acute injuries and chronic problems (asthma, eczema, headaches, and so on) and aids the breaking of addictions
- It helps to relieve pain
- It removes energy blockages and adjusts the energy flow of the endocrine system, bringing the body into balance and harmony
- It assists the body in cleaning itself of toxins
- It reduces some of the side-effects of drugs, and helps the body to recover from drug therapy after surgery and chemotherapy
- It supports the immune system
- It increases vitality and postpones the ageing process
- It raises the vibrational frequency of the body
- It helps spiritual growth and emotional clearing

Energy healing works! It changes you from the inside out. The main thing to remember is that body, mind and soul, together with the energy body, form one invisible whole. Simple, non-invasive healing systems work with the Higher Self of the receiver to promote health and wellbeing of the entire physical, emotional, mental and spiritual body. Therefore energy healing is truly a system of attaining and promoting wholeness. It is an extremely powerful, yet gentle way to restore balance in your body. When this activity is combined with the sincere desire of the healer, who is willing to effect cleansing within their consciousness, then total healing can occur. A whole *new* you will in time emerge!

Types of Energy Healing

In this section I mention some of the most popular energy-healing modalities or alternative medicine, which range from ancient Chinese medicine to Indian forms. I practise some of these therapies in my clinic. When you visit a holistic practitioner, make sure it is someone reliable and that they have accredited certification by the respective bodies or organization.

Energy healing is an effective way to work with the imbalances in your energy body. There is currently a wide range of different holistic modalities, some more popular than others, and it is important to mention that not all of them are suitable for everyone. It really depends on what you are trying to achieve, how much time you have, and so on.

Below I will explain three types of energy healing that are very popular right now, but feel free to do research in your local area for holistic practitioners and to try out the healing method that best suits your needs. Now that you have a bit more knowledge about your chakras and the energy body, you will see a new world of energy healing opening up in front of you.

In this book we will cover Reiki, colour therapy and crystal healing. I have chosen these three methods because they are very straightforward and easy to use yourself at home, compared with acupuncture, for instance, which requires a qualified practitioner to carry out the therapy on you.

Reiki

Reiki is a Japanese technique for stress reduction and relaxation, which also promotes healing. It is a simple, natural and safe method of spiritual healing and self-improvement that everyone can use. Reiki is a gentle therapy that complements traditional medicine, and is considered to be part of complementary and alternative medicine (CAM). It doesn't have any contraindications, and it works on the basis that we are all energy beings and have an energetic or subtle body.

Colour Therapy

Colour therapy consists of utilizing the energy of the light – using colours to heal physically, mentally and emotionally. We are surrounded by colours, and we live from day by day with them: the colours we get from the light of the visible spectrum of the Sun, like the ones that are in a rainbow. Those seven colours are present every day in different shades and combinations. When vibrating, these colours will show us a state of mind and will even affect some bodily organs – the skin, for example.

Crystal Healing

Crystals are *medicina* from Mother Earth. The word *medicina* is of shamanic origin and means everything that Mother Earth gives us to heal ourselves and recover our physical, mental and emotional health. Mother Earth provides us with plants and medicinal herbs in the natural kingdom, and in the mineral kingdom Mother Earth gives us crystals and gems. Crystal healing is about using these natural resources to recalibrate the body's vibrational frequency. Crystals can store, absorb and transmit energy.

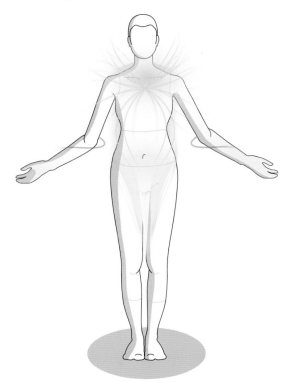

"I am ready to be showered with an influx of cosmic high-vibrational energies. I will allow those energies to flow in every part of my body."

Reiki

Reiki practitioners channel energy through their hands in a particular pattern to heal and harmonize the natural energy field of a person. Reiki uses traditional and ancient symbols to channel this energy into the recipient's body. It works on humans, animals and plants, as it involves the universal life-force energy, which sustains life and promotes healing in all living things.

This therapy is a gentle, non-invasive form of hands-on healing. Reiki healers channel the ki of the universe so that a person heals. Reiki is becoming very popular among both men and women, due to its incredible physical, mental and emotional benefits. While Reiki is not a religion, it is still important to live and act in a way that promotes harmony with others and with the planet.

Some of the benefits of Reiki include:
- It brings deep relaxation
- It releases energy blockages
- It detoxifies the subtle-energy system
- It balances the chakras
- It provides new vitality
- It increases the vibrational frequency of the body
- It reduces stress levels
- It helps to reduce anxiety

There are no limits to Reiki, because it flows wherever it is needed the most. However, the recipient's willingness to cast off old habits and patterns, to accept change and healing has to be present during the session. This therapy can be done face-to-face or by distance healing, as Reiki energy can travel through time and space; the healing takes place in the quantum realm and not in the physical realm. Reiki energy is free and available to everyone, so in theory you are able to give yourself a Reiki self-treatment.

If you are interested in Reiki, it is likely that you have been guided on your healing journey to many places and experiences in the past, and now find yourself at your current place as you continue to explore the possibilities for deep healing and inner discovery. Mikao Usui, the Japanese founder of the Reiki system of natural healing, recommended that people practise certain simple ethical ideals to promote peace and harmony that are nearly universal across all cultures, and these are known as the Reiki principles.

Caution: Reiki should never be used instead of medical treatment. It should always be done as a complementary therapy and as a way to become, and remain, healthy.

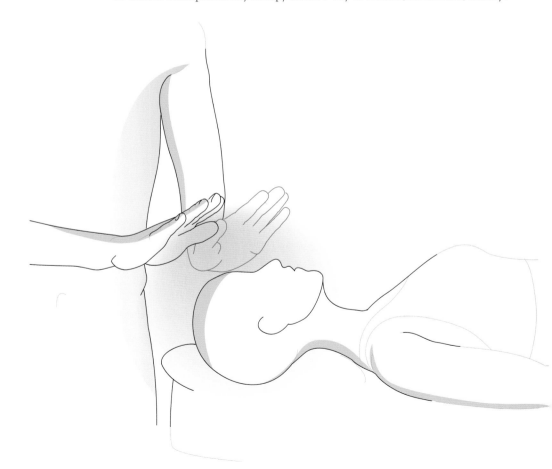

Reiki Chakra Self-balance

This exercise offers you an effective way to balance the chakras with a Usui Reiki self-healing method. By aligning your chakras in this way you are recalibrating each one of them and releasing energy blockages within them. When we are able to dissolve those blockages, we are allowing the life force to flow freely in the body. After this session you should feel grounded, more heart-centred, uplifted, liberated from repressed feelings, relaxed, empowered and loved.

Choose a day and a time that are good for you to receive Reiki, and when you know you won't be disturbed during the session. Wear comfortable clothes. Cleanse the space energetically (see page 194). Keep a glass of drinking water near you. Wash your hands. You can apply essential oils, light a candle or play relaxing music if you wish. These are all optional; all you really need is yourself and your intent to receive Reiki.

Duration: 30 minutes

1. Start by cleansing yourself energetically. Standing on bare feet with your legs slightly apart (if you are unable to stand up, you can sit on a chair with both feet firmly on the floor, but avoiding crossing your legs), commence cleansing your aura gently. Beginning on the left side and raising your left arm to shoulder level, start aura-combing (see page 54) with your right hand, about 5cm (2in) above your skin, from your left shoulder to your left fingers: above and below, inner side and outer side. Repeat this movement for few strokes, then repeat on your right side. Then move to the top of your head, and again use brushing movements from your head to your feet: at the front of the body first and then at the back.

2. Once you have finished cleansing your aura, take a few deep inhalations and exhalations, raise your arms above your head with the palms facing up, and imagine strong healthy roots coming out of your feet and going down to the centre of the Earth. Visualize your roots tangling and anchoring in the core of the Earth while absorbing energy from the Earth. Feel Mother Earth's energy travelling all the way up your body from your feet, expanding in your whole body.

3. See the Earth energy activating your chakras as it moves up through your spine to the top of your head. Imagine Sahasrara activating and opening up, ready to receive the universal life force. Invoke the Reiki energy and any spiritual beings, ancestors, masters or angels you would like to assist you in your healing.

4. Imagine the Reiki energy as a golden light descending from the universe to Sahasrara and your hands, penetrating and filling your body with this healing bright energy, then mixing with the energies from the Earth travelling up and down your legs, torso, arms, hands and your entire being.

5. Bring your hands downs, rub your palms together until you can feel some heat, then start the Reiki healing. Placing your left palm on Muladhara and your right palm on top of your head, stay here for few breaths, bringing your attention to Muladhara and Sahasrara. Imagine the Reiki energy as golden light coming out of the palms of your hands and healing these two chakras.

6. When you are ready, move your left hand to Svadhisthana and your right hand to Ajna, and repeat the same action.

7. Once you are ready, place your left hand on Manipura, 7.5cm (3in) above your navel centre, and your right hand on Vishuddha. Again imagine the golden light radiating from your hands and healing your chakras.

8. When you feel ready, bring both hands, one on top of the other, to Anahata. Visualize the Reiki energy healing this chakra. Stay here for as long as you need to.

9. Once you are ready, bring your awareness to Sahasrara and imagine the flower on top of your head closing up. Then start drawing your roots up and up from the Earth, until they get back into your feet. When you have finished, join your palms together in the Prayer Position in front of your chest. Thank the Reiki energy for healing you, and thank the beings from other dimensions that you called on to assist you in your healing. Acknowledge that the healing took place and for that you are grateful.

10. Take a gentle bow with your head. The session is finished.

Colour Therapy

When we are doing colour therapy, we are trying to harmonize the food we eat, the clothes and accessories we wear and the rooms we are in, and it's important to take into account of the colours that attract us and those we like most. Scientifically and sensitively, it is proven that colours manifest certain attitudes in our bodies. In a hospital, for instance, green or blue can bring a certain tranquillity; and the colours of a restaurant can motivate us to eat. This is how colours encourage us to take certain actions or to adopt a specific emotional attitude toward something.

There are different healing methods to use with colour therapy. Some people use bottles of water that are exposed to the sun, wrapped in the colours of nature (the colours of the rainbow), which vibrate in the light and radiation of the Sun. This water must be drinkable, so that you can drink it afterwards and get all the benefits of the energy of the light spectrum and of that colour vibration.

There is also colour therapy using crystals, the food we eat, the clothes we wear and the rooms we are in. This kind of holistic therapy can be used in our daily lives. For example, the colours in the food that we eat every day manifest different qualities: red foods activate the blood's circulation; when we eat yellow foods we stimulate the digestive process; orange foods detoxify and purify; blue foods help us to increase our defences and potentiate the immune system; the green colour of vegetables and salad leaves leads to regeneration.

Colour Meanings

- **Red**: Muladhara is governed by this colour. It represents our ties to the Earth and always shows a positive outlook. Red promotes strong qualities of courage, security and self-confidence. It stimulates and energizes the wearer. It can help when you are tired, anaemic, need courage or simply renewed energy. This colour is also associated with sexuality, passion and power.
- **Orange**: Svadhisthana is ruled by this colour. Orange is stimulating and helps us in times of depression and loneliness. It also has love from the colour red, and wisdom from the colour yellow, mixed into it. Orange will help the wearer increase their appetite, and will assist with nerves, asthma and allergies. It also helps when you lack the energy to do the work you need to get done.

- **Yellow**: Manipura is associated with this colour and is often referred to as the brain of the nervous system. When this chakra is balanced, we shouldn't have any abdominal problems. It helps to cleanse the pores in the skin and stimulates the brain. Yellow is compared to joy and brightness. It may help when you are tired, depressed, have skin or weight problems or suffer from ulcers. This colour is also associated with fire and action.
- **Green**: Anahata is ruled by this colour. Green has a harmonizing energy and helps with balancing. It has a very strong tie to nature and can help the wearer become peaceful and have more harmony in life. Green can also help to calm your nerves, assist with migraines, and help when you have a need for peace and tranquillity or require positive and happy feelings. The colour green is healing.
- **Blue**: Vishuddha is powered by blue energy. Blue represents spirituality and is a great healing power. It can help calm your mind, assist with sleep, a fever or when you have a major shock in your life. Its calm nature keeps us connected with the universe. Light-blue colours are very relaxing and calming, so wear this colour in moments of stress.
- **Indigo**: Ajna is associated with this deep-blue energy. Indigo is a sedative and helps to open our intuition. It is a colour that is calming to both the nervous system and the lymphatic system. It stimulates the flow of subtle energies throughout the psychic centres and the nervous system. Indigo is the colour of divine knowledge and the higher mind.
- **Violet**: Sahasrara is governed by this colour. The violet energy connects us to our spiritual self, bringing guidance, wisdom and inner strength. It is the colour of spiritual protection and transformation and is associated with the divine. It has a very calming effect on us and is, therefore, helpful for those people who are experiencing sleep difficulties or stress.

Colour Therapy: Chakra Balance Using Water

I learned this chakra balance using just water from my mum, who is a firm believer in the power of intentions, words and blessings. As water is so vital to us, and human beings are made up of 60–70 per cent water, she changes the patterns of crystals in the water by raising the vibration of the water before drinking it. She used to put up sticky notes with positive affirmations or healing messages, then leave the water overnight and drink it the next day.

As I work with the chakras, I have added the colours. But you can make this exercise your own and use it in any way that works for you.

Duration: 7 days (one chakra each day)

You will need: seven pieces or small sheets of coloured paper in red, orange, yellow, green, light blue, indigo and violet (or white); a jug of water (preferably of transparent glass); a pen

1. On a Sunday night before going to bed, fill your jug with fresh water and place the red piece of paper underneath the jug. You can write a positive affirmation or quality related to Muladhara (see page 285) that you would like to bring more of into your life. For example, "I am grounded", "I feel supported and protected" or "I have everything I need in my life" – write a word, a phrase or anything that feels right to you. Leave it overnight.

2. On Monday morning, as soon as you get up, tune into your intention and connect with it. Imagine that the water in the jug has absorbed all the power and healing benefits of the colour red. Drink the water slowly and with intention. Visualize it cleansing you as it passes down your throat behind your sternum into your stomach. Imagine the red water flushing away the negative emotions from Muladhara. The water is cleansing you, and your entire system, of unwanted negative energy. Close your eyes while drinking the water – that really helps you to stay connected with your inner self and experience the sensations of this chakra healing. Keep drinking this water throughout the day, using the same methodology.

3. On Monday evening do the same you did on Sunday evening, except this time use the orange paper, as you will be connecting to Svadhisthana. Write down some Svadhisthana affirmations (see page 286). The next day, Tuesday, do the same as you did with the red-charged water.

4. Repeat this procedure each day for each chakra, remembering that you need to prepare the night before.
- Wednesday: Manipura, yellow colour
- Thursday: Anahata, green colour
- Friday: Vishuddha, light-blue colour
- Saturday: Ajna, indigo colour
- Sunday: Sahasrara, violet colour

Tips: Try to drink the water at the same time each day, if possible. You are recalibrating and reprogramming your energy body. You know how, when your doctor prescribes your medication, he or she advises you to take it at the same time each day? The same thing applies here. And if you don't want to do the whole chakra balance in a week, you can focus on one particular chakra for three days, depending on what you would like to achieve.

Crystal Healing

Mother Earth provides us with everything we need to heal ourselves: minerals, food, plants, medicinal herbs and crystals. Crystal healing is a holistic and natural therapy for energy healing that uses the power of crystals, natural stones and minerals as a conduit to tap into the energy of the chakras and our electromagnetic field.

Crystals can help us in two ways:
- **Vibration of the crystal**: With their high-vibrational frequency, crystals have a unique ability to balance our chakras and our energy field. Quartz crystals, for example, have the highest emanation of high-vibrational frequencies, and this is why we use them as healing crystals.
- **Colour of the crystal**: We use crystals for their colour, which affects our chakras because their vibration emanates colour. An effective cure has the power to create stability at an energetic level, and reinforcement on a chromatic (colour-related) level. For this reason we can wear crystals or put them on our body for crystal healing over every energy centre. We can use minerals of the same colour as the chakras, and this creates stability and is used as a very successful medicine.

We can use crystals in our favourite colour, enjoy crystals as an ornament or bring them into our homes to achieve balance within our space. We can use them to meditate and relax. If we have a special connection that we feel in our heart, and a certain crystal attracts us – a particular colour or shape – then simply feeling that, and resounding with the crystal's energy, amplifies its effectiveness even more.

Clear crystals help us to have a greater connection with ourselves and who we really are: moving further from our ego and our personality, toward our true character and personal nature. Merely wearing a crystal is not enough, though. To use its power as a remedy – as a medicine – it is recommended that you have constant contact with it, on your body: put it near your heart, or in a bag with other shamanic medications. Furthermore, you must integrate its vibration.

I find that wearing a crystal as a necklace is a very effective and practical way to absorb its energy, because it resonates with the most powerful instrument we have – our heart. We can also wear crystals on our wrists, or on our hands as a ring, because we are always moving our hands. According to the Tantras, our body has 72,000 *nadis* or energy channels, which are electromagnetic, and around 114 chakras, and they are constantly interchanging, absorbing and emanating energy, so when we hold a crystal or place a crystal on our body there is a positive exchange of energy there. This is how the crystal healing takes place.

Among the three kingdoms of the planet Earth (the animal, vegetable and mineral kingdoms), the only one that is stable, and outside the laws of time, is the crystal kingdom. Crystals last forever, especially those belonging to the quartz family, which can be owned and passed on from generation to generation. They don't change, they regulate themselves automatically, and they fix themselves, because they have been created, developed and grown in the interior of the Earth – in the guts of Mother Earth – and hold the Earth's DNA imprint.

Disease and illness are created due to a low-vibrational body and have a great percentage of stagnant negative energy, and this is what causes pains in the human body at a particular moment. Placing crystals on the chakras, holding them or wearing them, can help to raise low energies up to a higher vibration and release those energy blockages. Meditation, visualization and colour therapy are all excellent ways to balance the chakra system at home. Many people find crystals and semi-precious stones helpful in focusing and balancing their chakras.

The list on the next two pages is an overview of some common ailments and the crystals that can help to alleviate them. You can meditate with all these crystals, whether by holding them in your left hand, placing them on the related chakra, wearing them as jewellery, having them around your home or placing them under your pillow.

Caution: Please seek help from a qualified practitioner if you need medical attention.

USING CRYSTALS TO HEAL

Anxiety
Black tourmaline (grounding)
Danburite (comforting)
Blue-lace agate (calming and soothing)
Sodalite (calming the mind)
Amethyst (attracts positive energy)
Shungite (helps release negative energy)
Fluorite (understanding)
Haematite (grounding)

Depression
Rose quartz (stimulates self-worth and inner peace)
Sunstone (radiates positive energy)
Lepidolite (stabilizes mood)
Smoky quartz (grounding)
Pink opal (heals emotional pain)
Carnelian (motivation)
Tiger's eye (strength)
Rutilated quartz (uplifting)

Stress
Blue-lace agate (calming)
Black jasper (calming and grounding)
Sodalite (calming the mind)
Rhodonite (centring)
Amazonite (balance and harmony)
Clear quartz (cleansing and balancing)
Shungite (releases negativity)

Weight Loss
Yellow jasper (motivation and willpower)
Lodolite (manifestation, amplifies intentions)
Sunstone (uplifting, keeps positive energy)

Yellow apatite (aids poor digestion, eliminates toxins)
Lolite (releases fatty deposits)
Gaspeite (stimulates metabolism)

Grief
Pink calcite (promotes inner peace)
Amethyst (transition/transformation)
Black onyx (grounding, inner strength)
Rose quartz (unconditional love, soothing)
Clear quartz (master healer for physical and emotional pain)
Moonstone (grounding, soothing)
Pink opal (calming, relieves stress)

Fears
Black tourmaline (grounding, protective)
Labradorite (inner wisdom)
Haematite (mental strength)
Aquamarine (calming, serenity)
Blue-lace agate (centring, calming)
Black onyx (alleviates worries)
Garnet (general fears, insecurity)

Immune-system Boosting
Amethyst (cleansing, balancing)
Ametrine (strengthens immune system)
Carnelian (vitalizer, purifies)
Aquamarine (alleviates triggers)
Bloodstone (purification)
Brown jasper (clears toxins)
Green aventurine (fights flu symptoms)
Malachite (boosts immune system)

Chakra Balance with Crystals

I personally prefer flat or palm-shaped crystals for chakra balancing, as they are easy to place on the body and are just the right size. Using tumbled crystals (smooth or round ones with a polished appearance) might be a little challenging, as they may roll off your body. Make sure that your crystals are cleansed (you can do this under running water, imagining all the negativity being washed away; pass them over the smoke of incense, sage or sacred wood; or bury them in the soil) and ready to be used for healing. After cleansing my crystals, I normally I charge them, by placing them in the sunshine or in moonlight from the full Moon.

Caution: Be aware that some crystals, like selenite, can dissolve in water. Not all crystals are suitable for cleansing in water.

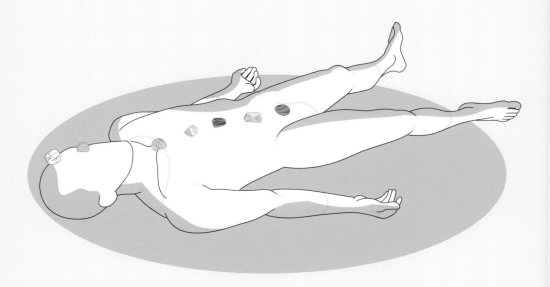

Duration: 20 minutes

You will need: each of the following crystals
- 1 Muladhara crystal = jasper, bloodstone, smoky quartz, black tourmaline
- 1 Svadhisthana crystal = carnelian, orange calcite, citrine, amber
- 1 Manipura crystal = yellow tiger's eye, citrine, yellow jasper, yellow tourmaline
- 1 Anahata crystal = green aventurine, rose quartz, emerald, amazonite, green jade
- 1 Vishuddha crystal = blue-lace agate, blue chalcedony, turquoise, sodalite, azurite
- 1 Ajna crystal = amethyst, clear quartz, lapis lazuli, azurite, fluorite, sodalite
- 1 Sahasrara crystal = clear quartz, amethyst, lemurian, selenite

1. Find a quiet place, lie down and make sure you are in a comfortable position. Start by placing your crystals on your chakras, one by one, starting with Muladhara and finishing with Sahasrara on the top of your head.

2. Once you have finished placing all seven crystals, close your eyes and take few deep inhalations and exhalations. Surrender to whatever is, and enjoy the stillness. Focus on your breath, relax and let the crystals do their work. Stay here for at least 20 minutes.

3. When you feel ready, very gently remove the crystals, starting from the top of the head and moving down to Muladhara.

4. Keeping your eyes closed, turn your body to one side, inhale and slowly push yourself up. Sit for a couple of minutes. Feel the sensations in your body. When you are ready, stand up.

Energy and Aura-cleansing

Energy cleansing – or energy hygiene, as some people call it – is very important because whatever is going on in your energy body affects your physical body, and this in turn affects the physical space you are in. If you are picking up negative energies in your energy body because the collective is experiencing a lot of fear and anxiety, those energies will add up in your energy body and eventually will affect your physical body and will be reflected in your surrounding space, too.

Everything is connected. Your subtle body, your energy body (that is, your chakras), your aura and the *nadis* or meridians, which are the energy pathways in your body, are all connected. The physical body and the energy body are constantly communicating with each other. That is why energy hygiene is so important – just like washing your hands to keep them clean and to remove dirt and germs that can potentially make you sick.

Clearing and cleansing that unwanted energy from your subtle body and your energy body – and from your space – regularly is going to be very helpful and is probably going to make you feel better, too! There are many different ways to cleanse your energy, but before we get to that, I would like to tell you about the process. This is something I have learned from my mother, from my own personal practice and from my research.

The first part of the process is to give yourself enough time for this activity. Make sure that you allow at least 15–30 minutes for energy cleansing, so that you can dedicate enough time to it and don't feel you have to rush it. Choose a good day and time for you to do your energy cleansing. I normally do it on a Sunday, as it's such an easy day and I don't have much going on. You should go with whatever suits you best.

The next thing I'd like to recommend is cleaning your physical space. You can make this cleaning as superficial or as deep as you wish. It really depends on how you are feeling. But if your space feels clean and clear, obviously this is going to make you feel better energetically too. So whether if it's a simple declutter or a deep clean, dedicate some time to making you feel good about the space you are in.

Another thing I would like to recommend is doing some activity that gets your energy flowing – for example, playing your favourite music and dancing around for a bit; or a gym session, yoga class or even meditation: anything that gets you in the mood, but also increases your vibration and gets your energy flowing. Remember that your energy body can affect the energy of your physical space as well. This is a great way to start the cleansing process, both within yourself and within your space. Something I love doing, when energetically clearing my physical space, is playing loud mantras for healing or for clearing negative energy. You can find these easily on YouTube.

Last but not least, it is important to keep in mind that every time you clean your physical space, you have to make sure you have a plan for what you would like to bring into this space. Because if you clean everything away and don't bring anything positive in, it's quite likely that the space will eventually fill up with the same junk you just have cleared away.

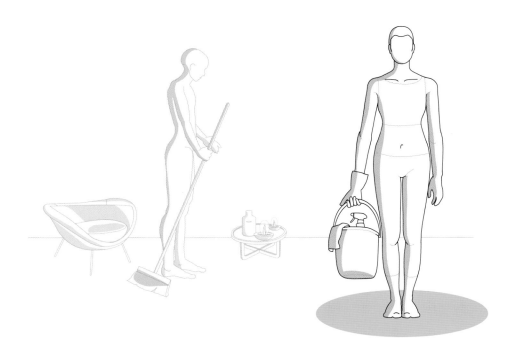

Tools for Energy and Aura-cleansing

The idea of using tools in energy healing is not a new thing – this is part of our heritage from our ancestors. They were communities that used to worship the Sun or the Moon, or spirits, and using different elements in their rituals or ceremonies would help them channel good energies. Nowadays we still continue with some of these traditions. It shouldn't surprise you when you visit a spiritual or energy healer and see all sorts of unusual items around the room. In a way these are the equivalent of a doctor's medical kit. Energy-workers need these tools to help them assess and carry out successful spiritual and healing activities. You have probably seen or heard about pendulums, crystals, Tarot cards, pentagrams, Reiki symbols, space-clearing sprays, sacred wood, oracle cards, candle magic, feathers, and so on. When it comes to aura-cleansing or space-clearing, such tools can be very handy and can reinforce the intention of the healing that is taking place, so that it becomes a ritual as well.

The following items or spiritual tools are commonly used in energy clearing and spiritual healing practices and can easily be used at home, so let's take a look at them.

Crystals

In the same way that crystals work on raising the vibration of your body, they can also help you to raise the vibration in your physical space. You can place crystals around your home, workplace or vehicle, depending on what type of energy you wish to bring into your space and your life. Most crystals have the ability to absorb, store and transform negative energy into positive energy.

Selenite is a great crystal to cleanse the aura. You can use a selenite wand to comb through your aura from head to toe, and the back and front of your body. This is one of the most popular crystals for energy cleansing; it is known as a neutral crystal, so it can also be used for healing, amplifying and protection. Selenite has the ability to cleanse itself, so there's no need to cleanse it yourself.

Herbs

Burning herbs, sage or charcoal is an ancient tradition. It is generally used to purify the space and the energy field of a person. Shamans believe that the smoke produced from burning these can get rid of bad spirits and darkness, while bringing healing benefits. The process is usually accompanied by prayers or chants.

You can buy white sage or palo santo (sacred wood) in any reliable spiritual shop, or you can make your own herb stick. It is really a personal preference. I particularly like using white sage or palo santo both in my space and on myself. Make sure that your space is well ventilated when burning herbs, as it can produce quite a dense smoke.

Caution: I would not recommend, under any circumstances, using this cleansing method around small children, pets, pregnant women or people with respiratory problems. There are other effective tools that you can use to clear their energy.

Space-clearing Sprays

I love space-clearing sprays. They are a straightforward, easy and practical way to clear negative energies without this being too obvious. They are great for workplaces, therapy rooms and vehicles. You can buy them online or in any good spiritual shop. Alternatively, you can make your own: all you need is a clean small-to-medium spray container, some table salt, a few drops of any essential oil and a small crystal quartz; mix it all up, add an intention to it and voilà! You have just made a space-clearing spray, which you can now use to cleanse any space that requires it.

Candles

Candles are really good to use when clearing energy from your physical space, because they not only represent a ritual, but the light that is the opposite to darkness. For space-clearing I like to use white candles because they are associated with purity, positive energies, purification, newness, hope and spirituality. You can walk around each room and visualize that the light of the candle is entering each corner. Candles are a great tool for bringing into your space whatever type of energy you want: for example, red candles are associated with passion, sexuality and love, so perhaps you feel like using that colour in your bedroom.

Candles have their own vibrational frequency, and this is why they have been used for centuries in rituals and ceremonies. If you want to learn more about candle magic, there are plenty books and information online, where you can take a look and learn a bit more about this fascinating ancient tradition.

Mantras

The great thing about mantras is that they can be used by anyone. All you need is your voice. Mantras are words or sounds that hold a high-vibrational frequency. They can be ancient Sanskrit mantras, such as "OM" or the word "Love". Whenever you are clearing your physical space – or yourself – of unwanted low-vibrational energies, you can easily use any mantra that resonates with you. Ideally you should inhale and, as you exhale, chant your mantra from Manipura several times. This will eventually raise not only your own vibration, but that of the space you are in.

Sound

Another great tool to use when clearing space is sound, because the right frequency can be very healing. You can use your hands to clap and move energy around the house, or to shift stagnant energies in corners and cupboards. You can also use your voice, healing music, tuning forks, gongs and drums. Sound-healing is now becoming very popular for energy and aura-cleansing, despite having been around for thousands of years.

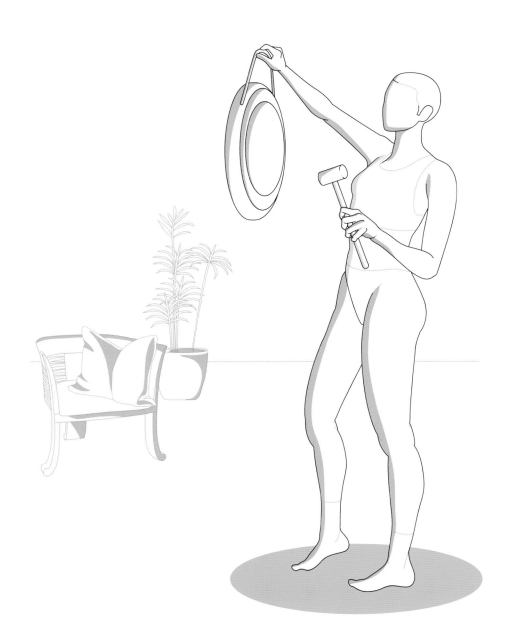

5

CHAKRAS
IN DAILY LIFE

Balancing Your Chakras at Home

If you want to live your life to the best, consider making some serious changes to your lifestyle, improving or incorporating new habits that can help you to achieve this. Most people chase happiness, good health, peace and balance throughout their lives, but unfortunately many of them are unable to fulfil this desire. I tell you this based on my own personal experience, as well as my studies and research.

Everything starts in the mind: this is your starting point. Scientific studies show that we have between 12,000 and 60,000 thoughts a day! Of those thousands of thoughts, 80 per cent are negative, and 95 per cent are exactly the same repetitive thoughts as the day before. These are incredible figures. In another interesting study, scientists found that 85 per cent of what we worry about never happens. And concerning the 15 per cent of worries that do happen, 79 per cent of those questioned discovered that they either handled the situation better than they expected or that the difficulty taught them a lesson.

We spend most of our lives worrying too much about things that won't happen! At some point in our lives we may realize that we need to direct our attention first to our minds, and there is no better medicine for the mind than meditation. The good news is that we are waking up and bringing more awareness to mental health.

This section of the book will give you the basic knowledge and tools to get you started on your healing journey at home. The practices described will help level up your consciousness and will enable you to discover yourself. So if you are not sure where or how to start your spiritual journey, this section is a good starting point. However, you need to have the right mindset to embark on this journey, so if someone told you that by placing a crystal on your forehead, everything was going to be okay, unfortunately they lied to you! Energy healing and chakra work require commitment, self-love and true intention.

There are many hurdles in day-to-day life that need overcoming, but it's liberating to know that stagnant energy can be released, so as to allow us to think and act more clearly and offer guidance to others. Chakras have been around for millennia and it is no wonder they are becoming more popular every day. Chakras empower us to take control of our health and wellbeing in a more spiritual and holistic way.

Start by creating your sacred space at home. It doesn't matter if all you have is an old rug or a cushion, or simply a lamp. Believe me when I say that your sacred space will evolve with you. It will represent your spiritual growth, and that's one beautiful thing about being on this journey.

Once you have created your sacred space, establish your regular meditation practice. Meditation will help you obtain the right mindset to start your journey toward a happy and a balanced healthy life. From there, you can move on to using mudras and yoga asanas in your daily life, practising traditional Kundalini Tantra and saying healing affirmations for the chakras.

Working with your chakras daily should be a reason for excitement, because at some point when you are more in tune with them, great things will come your way. Doors start opening, you will feel more balanced and happy, less stressed and more healthy – and all because you decided one day that enough was enough and took control of your mind, body, Spirit and wellbeing.

Balancing your chakras at home is very simple. Don't feel overwhelmed, thinking that you should already be a chakra guru after having read this book. Be patient, and start learning and understanding what your body and your mind need.

Sacred Space

Our home is our most sacred physical space – it gives us protection, refuge and is our cave – and we should have a sensation of comfort, serenity and peace there. Creating an altar in your home is going to help you find all these qualities.

An altar is a sacred space that connects us with the divine and gets us in sync with the universe, with the Earth and with ourselves. It is a source of positive energy that emanates light and blessings around our entire home. By having an altar at home, you are creating a very special space like an oasis, which, just by looking at it, is going to transmit calm and serenity and the sensation everything will be okay. It can also help if you are finding it difficult to establish or stick to your spiritual practice or meditation. You have something physical that you can see and touch, so the practice is not an abstract one. Once you manage to sit at your sacred space or altar for a few minutes for a few days a week, you are doing amazingly. You will already be shifting your body frequency, your thoughts will become more positive, and you will be slowly and gently realigning the chakras. The first step toward anything is always the hardest step. Just by sitting in silence in your sacred space you are shifting your thoughts and therefore the chakras.

What will the purpose of your sacred space be? Will you be sitting there solely for meditation or will you be practising an activity such as yoga there? It is necessary to ask yourself this question before you start creating your sacred space, because you need to consider the size of the area in question.

Once you have determined the size of your sacred space and its purpose, choose the room in your home where you will place your altar. Try to choose a cosy, quiet room, with natural light and good ventilation if at all possible.

Select the objects that you would like to have on your altar: crystals, candles, cushions, a rug, family photos, flowers, angelic figurines, and so on. Usually these are objects that connect you with the sacred, the divine, and therefore they should be special to you. Once you have selected your items, make sure that you cleanse them energetically. You can use palo santo, white sage or an incense stick to cleanse them, by waving the smoke around the objects, then add your intention that they should be cleansed of all old and negative energy, to get them in sync with the spiritual intention that you wish to create for your altar.

You may wish to integrate the five elements (Earth, Fire, Water, Air and Ether) in your altar and sacred space.

To represent the Earth element you can add a plant, rocks, stones, minerals, flowers, pine cones, wooden items and other objects that you collect from nature.

For the Fire element, you can add a candle.

For the element of Water you can include aquatic plants or a small glass or container of water.

For the element of Air you can add chimes that move with the wind and produce lovely soothing sounds, or small air instruments and an incense stick.

The element of Ether signifies the unity of all five elements; it represents the space but also love and unity. You can add a photo of an angel or item that represents love and union. Lastly, you can arrange the items of each element in their natural order in the cardinal points, and by doing this you are integrating Ether: Earth element = north, Fire element = south, Water element = west, Air element = east, and in the centre is Ether.

Once you have your space cleansed energetically, its purpose established and all your items in position, you need to activate the space and your altar. Activating the altar is very simple, but is an important part of creating your sacred space: declare loudly and clearly the intention of that space, to yourself and anyone else who is in contact with it. You can say a prayer or play nice music – basically it is like a small opening ceremony. I remember that every time my mother had a new altar in the house, she would decorate it with lots of flowers, there would be candles, incense and essential oils burning, and she would invite her close friends and family to attend the opening ceremony. It was like a little party. Knowing my mum, I guess it was an excuse to create a spiritual gathering, bringing people together to celebrate good health, light and love.

Spend some time in your altar space. Use it. Attend your altar with love and care. Enjoy it!

Spiritual Journal

A spiritual journal is a great way to track how you are growing spiritually. It is a wonderful tool that enables you to open up a little more and observe yourself at an honest and much deeper level. A spiritual journal offers you the opportunity to see how you are interacting not only with yourself, but with all those around you. This type of journal is different from a typical diary, in that you focus on the self and how you can align more with your true purpose. With a spiritual journal you can cultivate the practice of writing down your thoughts and feelings for the purpose of self-reflection and self-growth. It can help you become who you wish to be.

Since I've been journaling I've a noticed an increase in my creativity. Words seem to come out easily now, and it has helped me to express myself better, to understand myself and to comprehend why I interact with myself and others in the way I do. Journaling has assisted me in many different ways – emotionally, mentally and spiritually – and I'm glad this type of writing is becoming more popular and quite trendy nowadays. I believe this is due to the spiritual revolution that is currently blooming. Many people are seeking answers, and are keen to explore the self at a much more profound level. There is an increase in spiritual learning and spiritual healers, and in general there is a rising of the collective consciousness.

A spiritual journal can play an important role in someone's general wellbeing. I support and encourage such self-analysis and self-reflection. It is the only way we can grow as individuals, learn from our mistakes and do better in the future. Journaling offers us the opportunity to slow down and be present with ourselves. A spiritual journal can also help you open yourself up to all the chakras, but particularly to Sahasrara, which is the energy centre of connection with your spirituality.

How to Start a Spiritual Journal

If you haven't done this before and don't know how to start writing, I recommend that you don't put pressure on yourself. Not knowing what to write at first is absolutely normal and okay. At the beginning it can be a little bit slow, but once you start writing and discovering your own way, then your thoughts and feelings will flow and it will come more easily to you.

When I first began writing my journal – and I mean the very first clean page – I wasn't sure what to write on it, so I decided to write about how I was feeling, physically, emotionally and mentally, at that very moment. That got me started. Just allow your pen to manifest whatever is inside you.

Duration: about 20 minutes

1. First you need to pick a topic: for example, your personal life, your professional life, your studies, your business, or simply a quality such as gratitude.

2. Choose your tools: a nice notebook, a pen, crayons and anything else you wish to use to decorate it and make it more personal and relevant to you.

3. Choose the place where you will be journaling. Ideally this will be a quiet, clean space without too much clutter.

4. Choose the day and time when you will be journaling. It doesn't have to take place every day, but regular journaling is a good practice. At least three times a week is ideal.

5. Allocate 20 minutes to this activity and try to stick to that.

6. Enjoy your journaling.

"I accept that I need to make some changes in order to manifest my dreams and live a healthier and happier life. I am ready to reclaim my power and embody the natural healer within me."

Meditation

When I was studying meditation in India, our guru asked the class, "Why do you meditate?" Everyone, including me, gave him pretty much the same answer: we meditate because we want to attain control of our mind and become more calm, relaxed and stress-free. Then he asked us to show him how we meditated, so we proceeded to demonstrate how we did this. After that he told us that we were not achieving all those things with meditation, because none of us were sitting correctly for meditation. He then said, "I don't know what it is you are doing, but whatever it is, my dears, it is *not* meditation." He then started his lecture by saying that 50 per cent of meditation is posture. If you are not sitting correctly to start with, how you are supposed to sit quietly and peacefully during your meditation?

As we have already explored, there are many different methods you can use to tap into the energy of the chakras. One of the most popular ways is visualization, which is achieved through meditation and the breath. You can effectively channel energy into the chakras by practising meditation, which relaxes the mind and nervous system; and all the physical, mental and emotional benefits that meditation and breathing offer then impact energetically on the chakras.

How to Meditate

How many times you have sat in your meditation posture and, within minutes, have started feeling uncomfortable – a twitch here and there, pins and needles and your back begins to hurt? Preparation for your meditation is important, starting with the room or space where you are going to meditate, which should be free of noise and distractions. Here I have added some guidance on how to sit correctly for meditation, and on the different postures.

Finding a Place to Meditate

One of the first things is to find a place where you can sit comfortably. It should also be somewhere you will experience as few distractions as possible. Distractions are not good when you are meditating, because they can keep you from developing your focus and concentration and can draw your mind away from everything, especially if you are a newbie. Keep it nice and simple, but real. Once you get the hang of meditating by keeping away the distractions, you can even do your meditation while riding on a train, bus or plane.

The Postures of Meditation

From ancient times until now, people have practised meditation because of its proven benefits. Incorporating meditation as part of your daily life can make a big difference to your attitude and your outlook on life. Meditation offers a wide list of physical, mental and emotional benefits and, because it is a procedure, it involves several steps as well as different postures. Different spiritual traditions and meditation teachers suggest or prescribe different physical postures.

Over the following pages you will discover some popular meditation postures:
- Cross-legged posture (see page 210)
- Seated posture (see page 211)
- Kneeling posture (see page 212)
- Lying-down posture (see page 213)

Cross-legged Posture

One of the most popular postures is the cross-legged position (Easy Pose), which has a more advanced pose known as the Lotus Pose (cross-legged, but with both feet on the thighs or above the groin). During meditation the spinal cord must be kept straight and tall, so slouching is not a good idea. When you sit straight, it encourages good circulation of what is called "spiritual energy", which is the life force and vital breath. In most spiritual practices like yoga, meditation and *pranayama*, the back must be straight. With practice you will find that tipping point when you know that your back is straight, but not tense.

Seated Posture

If you are unable to sit cross-legged, then you can sit on a chair with your bare feet flat on the floor. You should sit up, keeping your back straight and holding the spine and head in alignment, without leaning to left or right, and with the thighs parallel to the floor. Your hands should rest comfortably on the arms of the chair or on your knees, with the elbows slightly bent. Your chin should be slightly tucked in, so that you create a nice straight line from your sitting bones to the crown of the head. Your shoulders should be relaxed.

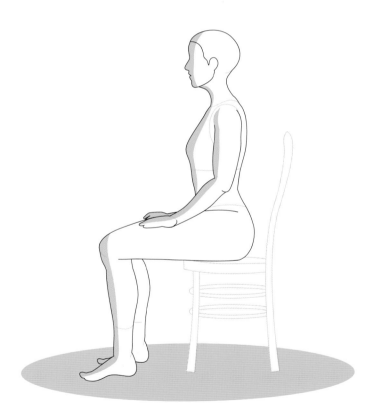

Kneeling Posture

Kneel with both knees on the floor and your buttocks resting on your toes and heels, which are almost touching. The hands should rest on the thighs. This position can be a little uncomfortable at first, as it stretches your ankles and thighs. There are some props that you can use to avoid discomfort: you can place a folded blanket or cushion under your knees, or under your feet or buttocks. Make sure that your back is nice and tall.

Lying-down Posture

This posture is also known as Corpse Pose or Savasana. You lie down on your back on the floor, keeping your legs straight and relaxed. The legs are hip-width apart, the arms away from the body, the palms of your hands face up and the back of your head touches the floor.

This posture is not used very often because it mimics the natural posture of sleeping, and the meditator can sometimes fall asleep. It is effective in reducing stress, rather than as a meditation process, so it's great for a bedtime meditation.

The Corpse Pose is a recovery and grounding pose, usually done at the end of a yoga class. It allows the nervous system to settle, the body to calm down and the heart rate to come to a natural pace. On an energetic level, Savasana helps the energies to integrate after a yoga class or energy-healing session.

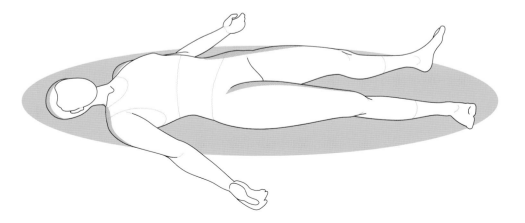

Incorporating *Mudras*

Mudras are hand (or body) gestures. Based on yogic philosophy, these gestures can affect our consciousness. One example is the common hand position of the Buddhist. The right hand rests on the top of the left hand with the thumbs touching, similar to the begging bowl of Buddha. *Mudras* unlock blocked energies or balance the masculine and feminine energies in our bodies, as well the five elements.

Repetitive Activities

Some meditators incorporate various repetitive activities in their stillness, such as humming, chanting or deep breathing, to help induce a state of meditation. These repetitions can last for a few minutes up to an hour. There are mantras that you can repeat continuously 108 times, or certain *kriyas*. I like these repetitive activities because they get you quickly into a meditative state and help you focus solely on that activity. They aid concentration on your meditation.

Duration and Frequency

The duration and frequency of meditation vary considerably. The broadly accepted duration is 20–30 minutes. This length may increase as the process goes on. To obtain the benefits of meditation, it is advisable to follow the advice and instruction of a spiritual teacher. Most traditions require daily practice, although some people may experience frustration or guilt when they fail to do this. Sometimes meditators complain about suffering from "meditator's knee", especially during long hours of kneeling or sitting cross-legged.

Bear in mind that perseverance and acceptance are needed to become successful at meditating. This may help you during prolonged hours of meditation and may increase the focus on your everyday life.

It may be challenging for most people to perform meditation as a daily habit, although it is not as difficult as some may think. There are several easy meditation techniques that anyone can perform on the path toward attaining a deeper sense of relaxation. Meditation is an effective weapon against banishing the stress brought on by the rigours of daily life. Start with few minutes a day and gradually increase the time. You will be surprised at how much your wellbeing can improve with just a few minutes of meditation a day.

Bija Mantra Meditation 1

A *bija* mantra meditation is a simple way to invoke sound vibrations in your body to harness the healing power of that energy. By chanting a specific mantra, you can tap into the underlying current of energy that exists in the universe. The seed mantra, or *bija* mantra, is a single syllable or word that holds high-vibrational frequency. Chanting a specific mantra helps us to get on that same frequency.

The correct way to chant a mantra is with the eyes closed, inhaling and chanting with the exhalation, loud enough that you can hear it and feel the vibrations in your body and in a particular chakra. You chant from the navel centre rather than from your throat. When chanting, you are calling up the energy from Muladhara to the throat. The energy travels through your spine and past Anahata. The *bija* mantras for the seven main chakras are as follows:

- Muladhara = LAM
- Svadhisthana = VAM
- Manipura = RAM
- Anahata = YAM
- Vishuddha = HAM
- Ajna = OM
- Sahasrara = OM/silence

Once you feel comfortable, close your eyes and start chanting and repeating the mantras to yourself. Let a mantra do whatever it wishes. If it is something that you wish to repeat slowly, fast, quietly or loudly, then do so. Try not to let outside thoughts disturb you while you are doing this. Just ignore them and focus on repeating your mantra.

As you repeat the mantra, be aware of what you are saying and focus on it, bringing your awareness to the relevant part of your body. Learn to remain relaxed and calm as you do this. You might sometimes find yourself going off on a daydream and stop repeating your mantra. Try to refocus and continue with your meditation before you veer off any further.

Start from Muladhara, continuing all the way up to Sahasrara, repeating each *bija* mantra seven times. Focus on deep inhalations and, as you exhale, let the chant come out. Once you have gone through all your chakras, take a few deep inhalations and exhalations before gently opening your eyes.

The key to this simple meditation is trying not to let distractions come before you as you meditate. It can sometimes be a bit hard to do this at first, but it will improve along the way and will help you better develop your focus and awareness. After some time, stop repeating your mantra and remain quiet while still sitting comfortably. Do this for a couple of minutes or so. Avoid getting up immediately after your meditation, which would be like jumping up straight after having a deep sleep. It would cause a lot of stress in itself.

The other key to making effective such easy meditation techniques is to perform them as a habit. Try to allow some free time in your schedule for your meditation. Making it a habit will improve your ability to keep away distractions when you do not need them. This meditation technique can be done in as little as 15 minutes or so. That is not such a long time to spend on something that can provide you with so many benefits.

The *bija* mantra meditation can also be done by chanting each mantra from the bottom Muladhara to the top Sahasrara, and vice versa, like an up-and-down system. Do this repetition several times, or for at least seven minutes. This clears up the energy centres and opens the chakras.

Bija Mantra Meditation 2

In this extended *bija* mantra meditation you chant seven cycles of the mantras.

Duration: 30 minutes

1. In a meditative posture bring your awareness to Muladhara and chant the mantra LAM while mentally feeling the vibration in that point.

2. Then bring your attention to Svadhisthana and repeat the mantra VAM.

3. Move your attention to Manipura and repeat the mantra RAM.

4. Then, at Anahata, repeat the mantra YAM.

5. Bring your attention to Vishuddha and repeat the mantra HAM.

6. Then move to Bindu chakra (instead of the usual Sahasrara, which is omitted here) and chant the mantra OM.

7. Now descend, repeating OM at Ajna.

8. Repeat HAM at Vishuddha.

9. At Anahata, repeat YAM.

10. Keep moving down to Manipura and repeat RAM.

11. Bring your attention to Svadhisthana again and chant VAM.

12. Come to Muladhara and repeat LAM. This makes one complete cycle.

13. Repeat all over again, for at least seven cycles.

14. You can finish by chanting three OMs to end your meditation. You should now feel refreshed, lighter, calmer and more balanced.

Chakra Visualization Meditation

Chakra meditation is about tapping into the energy of each chakra by visualizing its colour and bringing awareness into that part of your body. Learning how to do chakra meditation is easy, and everyone can do it. All you need is a quiet room where you won't be disturbed for at least 30 minutes and a little bit of imagination, and you're off.

You need to imagine a spinning light associated with each chakra. Start from Muladhara and work your way up to Sahasrara. You also need to know what colour of light is associated with each chakra, as follows:

- Muladhara = RED
- Svadhisthana = ORANGE
- Manipura = YELLOW
- Anahata = GREEN
- Vishuddha = BLUE
- Ajna = INDIGO
- Sahasrara = VIOLET or WHITE

At the beginning you might find difficult to visualize all the chakra colours. However, with regular practice you will be able to keep your mind focused on the chakras and their colours. When you sync your mind, breath and the energy centres, you bring alignment into your being.

Duration: 30 minutes

1. Start by finding a comfortable position, sitting with crossed legs or on a chair. Rest your hands on your knees. Close your eyes. Relax your shoulders and release any tension in your body. Bring awareness to your breath. Notice the quality of your breathing. Observe the breath flowing from your nostrils to your navel and back again. Take a moment to connect with your breathing.

2. Bring your attention to your body, from your head to your toes and from toes to head. Take a few deep inhalations through your nose, and deep exhalations through your nose.

3. Move your awareness to Muladhara, located at the base of your spine. Breathe in the colour red. Simply focus in that space, connect to the energy of Muladhara chakra and keep breathing consciously in and out. Imagine that as you breathe in you are expanding the colour red, and as you breathe out you are releasing old and negative energy from Muladhara.

4. When you are ready, bring your attention to Svadhisthana, which is located below the navel, on the lower abdomen. Bring the colour orange into that space. As you breathe into this energy centre you are feeling more and more connected to this area of your body. You see the colour orange expanding in this sacred space. Continue breathing in and out, releasing old emotions and feelings stored in this chakra.

5. When you are ready, bring your attention to Manipura. This chakra is located above the navel, just below your ribcage. Tap into the power of this energy centre by breathing the colour yellow into the centre of your belly. Keep breathing in and out, expanding the yellow colour even more and releasing old emotions and limiting beliefs as you breathe out. Stay here for few breaths.

6. When you are ready, come to Anahata. This is your heart centre and its colour is green. Again breathe deeply into this space of love and compassion. Allow the colour green to expand and emanate radiations of unconditional love and forgiveness. Take deep inhalations and exhalations as you imagine this heart centre becoming strong and radiant.

7. When you are ready, bring your awareness to Vishuddha. Breathe in the colour blue and visualize it expanding in your throat. Release any repressed emotions within this chakra. Let the blue light clear the emotional blockages you are holding in this area. Breathe in the new and breath out the old.

8. Now move your awareness to Ajna. Your third eye is on your forehead between your eyebrows. The colour of this energy centre is indigo. Keep visualizing a deep-blue colour growing and expanding in between your eyes as you breathe deeply into that space. Connect to your third eye, bringing clarity and vision into your being. Stay here for few deep inhalations and exhalations.

9. When you are ready, bring your attention to the
    seventh chakra, Sahasrara, which is located on the
    top of your head. This chakra has the ability to
    connect you to your Higher Self and the Source.
    The colour of this spiritual chakra is violet or white,
    so breathe any of these colours into your seventh
    chakra. Imagine the colour violet expanding on top
    of your head. Use your breath to tap into this area.
    Take deep, long inhalations and exhalations. Keep
    your eyes closed. Stay here for few more breaths.

10. When you are ready, visualize your entire body
    lit up with all seven colours from Muladhara to
    Sahasrara. Very slowly start bringing awareness to
    your body, taking a few breaths here before gently
    opening your eyes.

Drawing the Chakras

I love this practice and normally do it in my leisure time. Instead of watching television, I prefer drawing and colouring chakras and mandalas – geometric symbols of the universe. The creation of a chakra diagram should be done with absolute awareness and concentration. Remember that the chakras are psychic, so this is a fun way to connect with them and learn about them.

Play some nice relaxing music. I love tuning into Tibetan bowls or sound-healing, because this can enhance creativity and help with the internal healing process at the same time. It also helps you to concentrate and focus on what you are doing. This is a relaxing and uplifting activity to perform. By drawing the *yantra* of the chakras you are channelling their energy to your being. You are activating your brain to remember the symbols and figures; you are activating your sight; you are raising your vibration; you are using your hands, which are connected to your heart chakra, and you will easily remember this chakra when you are meditating; and your emotional body is being cleansed by this activity, which is therapeutic and healing.

There are plenty of books available that offer this method of relaxation and connection with mind, body and soul. Look out for pocket-size books as these are perfect to take on trips and road journeys.

Duration: as long as you wish

1. Choose one chakra that you are drawn to work with. Then gather all your materials together: pencils, crayons, paints, ruler, scissors, pens, and so on. Get a photo of the chakra you are drawing – you can get photos or pictures from the Internet – and do your best to replicate it.

2. Keep a pen and some paper nearby, so that you can journal any emotions that may arise during your activity.

3. Grab a cup of tea and enjoy the experience.

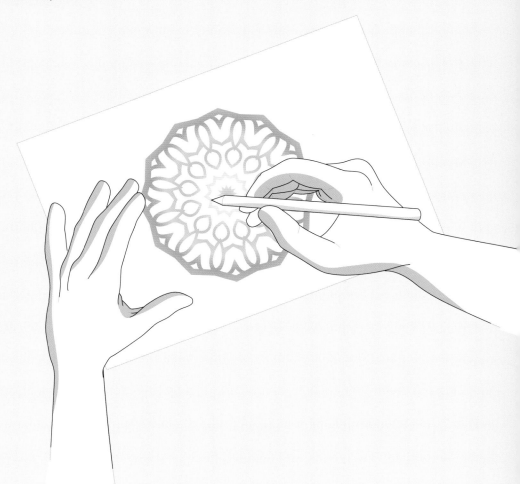

Chakra Yoga *Nidra*

Yoga *nidra*, also known as the yogic sleep, is a very deep, soothing meditation that alters your state of consciousness – while you are very relaxed, you are encouraged to remain awake during the meditation. Yoga *nidra* is usually a guided meditation and is proven to help relieve stress and restore physical, mental and emotional health. It is believed that when your mind is in such state of relaxation, healing takes place. The chakra yoga *nidra* focuses on the energy centres, to rebalance the chakras and bring harmony to the entire body; it works on a deeper level on the chakras, working with your subconscious and unconscious minds so that everything takes place in the emotional and mental bodies, which are areas that we don't normally explore consciously. Yoga *nidra* is very balancing and relaxing.

If you are able to record yourself reading this meditation script, or ask someone else to read it for you, that will be even better, as all you have to do is to lie down and listen to the meditation.

Make sure you are completely comfortable. If necessary, you can cover your eyes with an eye pillow or piece of cloth. If you fall asleep that's okay, it often happens when people start doing this meditation; the more you practise, the more awake and conscious you will remain during the practice.

Duration: 30 minutes

1. Lie down in Savasana or Corpse Pose (see page 213), then close your eyes. Look and feel the space in front of your closed eyes.

2. Bring awareness to your physical body. Notice the lightness of your body. Think of it as a leaf falling from a tree. Now slowly allow yourself to sink in the infinite space. Let go and surrender.

3. Observe the inflow and outflow of air in your body. Notice the rise and fall of the navel with each breath. Take a moment to set an intention in a short positive sentence. Repeat it at least three times and don't forget it.

4. Now visualize your own body from outside, as a third person. Allow yourself to relax even more and loosen each and every part of your body. Go through them in your mind, from your toes to the top of your head, and scan your body front and back.

5. Visualize your chakras from bottom to top, starting with Muladhara, then Svadhisthana, Manipura, Anahata, Vishuddha, Ajna and Sahasrara; and then from top to bottom, starting with Sahasrara, and then Ajna, Vishuddha, Anahata, Manipura, Svadhisthana and Muladhara.

6. Repeat your intention three times.

7. Slowly start bringing awareness to your physical body. Notice the sounds around you and the temperature of the room. Start moving your fingers and wiggling your toes. Bring your arms above your head and have a nice stretch.

8. Roll your body to one side. Take a deep breath and push yourself up to a seated position. Keeping your eyes closed, rub your hands together and place the palms on your eyes. Bring the hands down, then slowly open your eyes and come back to consciousness.

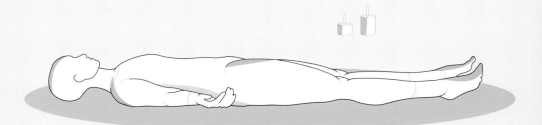

Scanning Your Aura with Your Hands

This is a very simple way to get you started on self-healing and experimenting with your own energy body, as well as learning to read the signs about what your body is trying to tell you. This exercise doesn't require much: just your hands and a little bit of time.

Using this scanning method you are activating your Ajna chakra and tapping into your intuition and inner guidance. Cultivate the practice of doing this aura scanning twice a week, or whenever you feel energetically heavy, stuck or emotionally confused.

Duration: 15–30 minutes

1. Find a quiet space. Wash your hands. Stand up with the feet slightly apart, or sit on a chair with your feet on the floor. Bring both your hands to your heart centre. Close your eyes.

2. Take a few deep inhalations and exhalations through your nose. And connect to your inner guidance. Ask the guru within to guide you and show you where in your body needs healing. Tap into that energy of wisdom within you. Feel it.

3. Rub your hands together until you have created some heat. With your right hand apply Jnana *mudra* (see page 235), and with your left hand start scanning your body from the top of the head at Sahasrara. Make sure you keep a distance between your hand and your body of around 10cm (4in) throughout the meditation. Continue to Ajna chakra, then Vishuddha, then move to Anahata. Continue doing the same with the rest of the chakras. Stay on each chakra for as long as you feel you need to.

4. Once you have scanned all seven energy centres you can stop there or, if you haven't picked up anything yet, you can do another round, starting again from the crown of your head. At first you might not feel or sense much, but with practice and over time you will be able feel those slight changes of energies within your aura. To give you an idea of what you are looking for, notice any hot or cold spots, any tingling feeling, any colour in your mind, or image, word or feeling.

Yantra Meditation

Yantras are ancient sacred symbols of immense power. They are geometric figures used for meditation and to gain high levels of consciousness. The practitioner focuses on a particular point of the symbol, which works as a window into the absolute. Just like mantras, *yantras* are very powerful tools that are designed purely for the purpose of worshipping a deity. Focusing the mind on one single point helps the monkey-mind to calm and achieve a high state of concentration.

Yantras are designed in such a way that the eye is carried into the centre of the sacred symbol. The *yantra* is a tool to channel energy as well; when meditating on a particular *yantra*, the mind can be tuned into the energy of the *yantra*, due to its vibration.

Duration: 15–30 minutes

1. Choose the chakra *yantra* of your choice. You can search for a *yantra* online and print it out.

2. Find a quiet space. Sit comfortably on the floor or on a chair. Keep your back straight. Place the centre of your *yantra* at eye level.

3. Gently take a few deep inhalations through your nose and exhalations through your mouth. Let the breath flow normally.

4. Focus your eyes on the centre of the yantra. Try not to blink, if possible. Keep your sight right on the centre and your eyes will naturally observe the whole *yantra*.

5. Repeat this every day. After a week or two you will be able to tap into the *yantra*'s energy even without looking at it.

Chakra Dance

Chakra dance is a way to awaken and activate Kundalini through body movement. It is a dynamic meditation, normally using nature sounds or tribal music while focusing on each chakra from Muladhara to Sahasrara. It enables you to release old energy and blockages by expressing your feelings and your emotional state. The chakra dance also cleanses and awakens the chakras while you tap into their energy and power.

Choose your preferred music or create a playlist for this dance. Start with some tribal sounds, with drums or rainforest noises for the lower chakras, then change to something more calming and less dynamic for the upper chakras, such as Reiki music, 432 Hz sounds or 528 Hz sounds. This dance is usually done with the eyes closed, as it is an internal journey. Some people like to put a bandage over their eyes so that they really immerse themselves in the experience.

Duration: 30–45 minutes

1. Find a quiet space or room. Wear light or loose clothing. Have a bottle of water next to you. Stand up firmly, with your legs slightly apart, arms by your sides and the palms of your hands facing forward. Close your eyes.

2. Take a few long, deep breaths. Relax your mind and body. Imagine strong, healthy roots coming out from the soles of your feet and penetrating the floor you are standing on. Visualize these roots penetrating the layers of the ground, travelling deep down to the centre of the Earth. Imagine the roots spreading out wide in the heart of the Earth and absorbing Earth energy.

3. Visualize this energy travelling through your roots all the way up to your feet, and from your feet visualize it spreading throughout your body to the top of your head. Feel that Mother Earth energy within you. You are feeling grounded and supported. Say in your mind or out loud, "I am grounded and supported."

4. Now, play your playlist, starting with the drumming and tribal music. Keeping your eyes closed and feeling the music in your body, bring your awareness to Muladhara. Start breathing into this energy centre. Visualize the red colour activating and expanding as you are tapping into this energy. Start moving your lower body – you may wish to open your legs wider and embody the Goddess Pose (see page 252) or stamp your feet and follow the beat of the drums. Create your own rhythm. Allow Muladhara to express and release emotional blockages. Keep breathing deeply into the chakra, embodying the element of Earth.

5. Do the same thing as you move to Svadhisthana and the element of Water. Here you may wish to start moving your hips from side to side and start bringing your awareness to this chakra. Imagine a bright-orange light expanding and activating. Keep moving and flowing with the music: bring sensuality into your dance, feel your body.

6. Move to Manipura and the element of Fire. Breathe into this chakra as you imagine a bright-yellow light activating and expanding within you. This is the chakra of energy and the self – the Sun in you. Embody Manipura qualities within your dance by become more dynamic and energetic; bring the Fire within you – roar if you feel like it. Let your body move however it wishes to.

7. Bring your awareness to Anahata (the music should now change to a more relaxing sound), then breathe into this space, imagining a bright-green light expanding and activating. This is the element of Air, movement and freedom. Move your arms – they are an extension of Anahata. Be as creative as you wish with your dance. Express the love of Anahata: you may feel like touching and hugging your body. Smile.

8. Bring your awareness to Vishuddha, the element of Ether and sound. Imagine the colour blue in this chakra activating and expanding with your breath. Keep dancing and expressing yourself.

9. Now move to the next chakra. Bring your awareness to Ajna and the element of Ether and Light. Imagine an indigo light in between your eyebrows expanding and activating. Continue dancing with gentle and soft movements before moving on to the last chakra.

10. Bring your awareness to Sahasrara and the element of Spirit. Imagine a violet light expanding and activating. Feel all your chakras radiating their light.

11. Keep dancing, coming to a stop slowly and gently. Keep your eyes closed. Stay here for a few breaths, just feeling the vibrations in your body and becoming aware of the sensations in it.

12. Now bring your attention back to your roots in the centre of the Earth and visualize them ascending through the Earth back to the soles of your feet.

13. Lie down for at least 10 minutes.

Chaturtha Pranayama

Chaturtha *pranayama* means "*pranayama* [breath control] of the fourth state".
This practice will lead to deeper awareness and knowledge of your chakras.
It is also a preparatory technique for *kriya* yoga and more advanced meditation
practices. Chaturtha *pranayama* is both a meditation practice and a breathing
practice, combining awareness of the breath, the universal sound OM and
the chakras.

There are four states of awareness, according to the Mandukya Upanishad.
 These are:

- Jagrat = waking state (external perception of the world)
- Swapna = dream state (perception of the subconscious mind)
- Sushupti = dreamless state (intuitive perception of the collective unconscious)
- Turiya = transcendental state (where words and definitions cannot reach).

Duration: 15–20 minutes

1. Sit in any comfortable meditative posture. Close your eyes and hold the back straight.

2. Breathe deeply in and out without breath retention (one round equals one inhalation and exhalation). Practise this for a few rounds, allowing the breathing to become deeper and more settled. Fix your awareness on the rhythmical flow of the breath.

3. The sound "O-o-o-o-o" should arise mentally with the inhalation. The sound "M-m-m-m-m" should arise with the exhalation. Both sounds are mental. Breathe through the nose, keeping your mouth closed. Continue in this manner, with awareness of the flow of the breath and the mantra.

4. Now focus your attention on Muladhara at the perineum. Feel that you are breathing in with the mental sound of "O-o-o-o-o". Feel the breath passing through the spine, piercing all the chakras: Muladhara, Svadhisthana, Manipura, Anahata, Vishuddha, Ajna and Sahasrara. Feel the breath and sound passing upward in the spine. On the exhalation, breathe out the sound "M-m-m-m", descending through the spine from Sahasrara to Muladhara. Feel the breath piercing all the chakras. This is the end of one round.

5. Do a few more rounds.

6. When you are ready, move to any of the chakras and continue the mental repetition of "OM" synchronized with the breath. Be aware of the mantra and the chakra only. Fill the chakra centre with the sound "O-o-o-o-o" and "M-m-m-m-m" as you keep breathing in and out.

7. Continue for a few rounds.

8. Start becoming aware of your body and your surroundings, and externalize yourself with the outer world. Slowly open your eyes.

"I breathe in peace, I breathe out fear. I breathe in the self, I breathe out the ego. I breathe in the new, I breathe out the old. Love and light fill me, fear and darkness leave me."

Mudras

The word *mudra* means "pleasure". It is also defined as a "seal" and a "shortcut". *Mudras* are symbolic gestures that are usually practised with the hands and fingers, although some *mudras* involve the entire body. They can also be described as psychic, emotional and devotional gestures that facilitate the flow of energy in the subtle body and enhance one's practice. By practising *mudras* you are cleansing your energy field and controlling the *prana* in your body.

The five elements in our hands are:
- Thumb = Fire
- Index finger = Air
- Middle finger = Akasha
- Ring finger = Earth
- Little finger = Water

Mudra Meditation

You can perform this meditation by sitting comfortably in a quiet space and holding any of these mudras for 5–10 minutes.

- **Jnana (Gyan)/meditation**: Index finger and thumb together. This helps to gain concentration.
- **Akasha/sky**: Thumb and middle finger together. This helps to alleviate ear disease.
- **Prithivi/Earth**: Thumb and ring finger together. This increases the Earth element within the body, stimulates and strengthens Muladhara and helps restore balance and stability in the body.

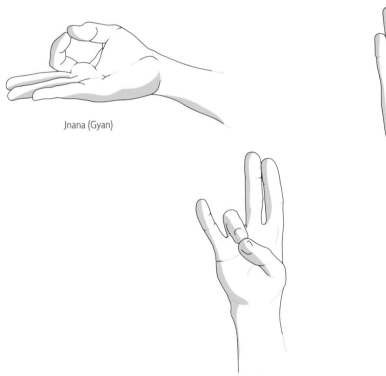

Jnana (Gyan)

Akasha

Prithivi

- **Agni/Fire**: Thumb pressing on ring finger's bone; the ring finger is bent, touching the palm of the hand. This improves digestion and helps the weight-loss process.
- **Varun/Water**: Thumb and small finger together. This balances water in the body.
- **Vyau/Air**: Tip of index finger at the base of the thumb. This is good for chronic and multi-disease and for the release of excessive gas, bloating and arthritis.

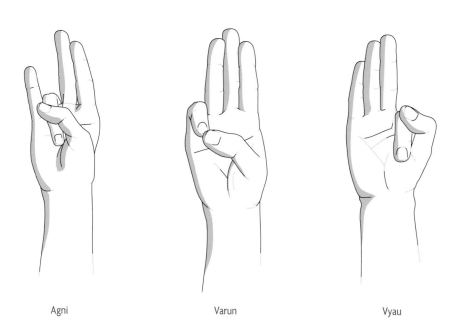

Agni   Varun   Vyau

- **Prana/vital energy**: Thumb, small finger and ring finger together. This stimulates *prana* air.
- **Apana/cleansing**: Thumb, ring finger and middle finger together. Apana air becomes activated. This helps to cleanse and detoxify the body.
- **Bhairava/balancing**: Right hand resting on top of the left hand. This balances the Ida and Pingala *nadis*.

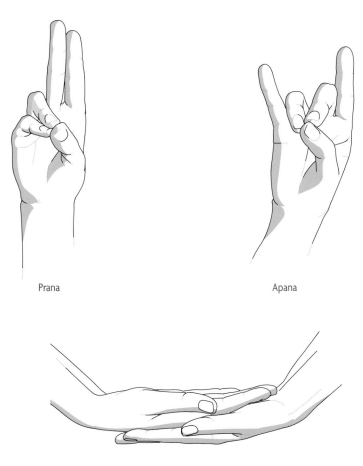

Prana

Apana

Bhairava

Yoga

Yoga is an ancient practice that is usually interpreted as an spiritual discipline bringing unity of the mind, body and Spirit. It is thought that the practice of yoga originated around 3,000 BCE in India in the Indus Valley, but it wasn't until many centuries later that Maharishi Patanjali, an ancient Indian sage, codified all aspects of yoga in his Sanskrit works, the greatest of which are the *Yoga Sutras*, which contain 196 verses and four chapters. Patanjali is also known as the "father of yoga".

A *sutra* can be defined as a short declaration or truth, so the *Yoga Sutras* are a concentration of truths that apply to anyone, regardless of their religion or culture. They are the truth of life because yoga is not just about stretching, breathing and holding poses; it teaches us how to live our lives in a balanced, happy and healthy way and how to deal with the challenges that we face daily. Yoga transforms us from the inside out. If you are only interested in the physical aspect of yoga (*asanas*), then you are missing out on a great chunk of goodness. With this book I would love to inspire you to deepen your yoga practice and see it as a philosophy of life. I invite you to use mantras, meditation and breathing exercises to amplify your spiritual practice and see the benefits in your wellbeing.

Yoga is the best way to stimulate and balance your chakras. Start slowly, bringing more awareness to your chakras when you are practising yoga. We tend to focus on the breathing a lot, especially if it's a fast pace of yoga such as Ashtanga or Vinyasa, but in a Kundalini or Hatha yoga class the focus will be on the chakras.

Yoga Poses and What They Achieve

Yoga is an incredible form of exercise for the mind, body and soul. I don't think there is anything else out there that can offer you as much as yoga does. Just imagining that this discipline was created thousands of years ago and we are in modern times, still incorporating this ancient wisdom into our lives, blows my mind away. Yoga is eternal and will stay with us until the end of days. In fact yoga practice is gaining more popularity and demand than ever before, due to people looking for spiritual growth and self-healing – and only yoga can offer you that, through its poses, meditation, *mudras*, mantras, *pranayama*, and so on.

Yoga poses have been designed to work on the chakras, as the energy centres in our bodies. Every time we practise yoga *asanas*, we are tapping into the energy of our chakras and into the energy body as a whole. Yoga poses also purify and cleanse our energy field. Yoga asks us to move our body so that we can release the toxins that make us sick. Through yoga *asanas* we can gain an endless list of physical, mental, emotional and spiritual benefits. Here are just some of them:

Physical Benefits of Yoga

- Increases flexibility and balance
- Improves the immune system
- Builds muscle strength and tones the body
- Maintains a balanced metabolism
- Prevents injuries and increases the elasticity in our joints
- Promotes a healthy spine
- Increases blood flow
- Improves the respiratory and digestive systems
- Regulates the adrenal glands

Mental and Emotional Benefits of Yoga

- Relieves stress
- Reduces anxiety and depression
- Calms the nervous system
- Increases body awareness
- Promotes mental balance
- Increases concentration
- Brings clarity of mind
- Builds self-confidence
- Increases mental and emotional awareness
- Helps discover our life purpose
- Helps to lessen addiction
- Reduces anger
- Makes us happier
- Brings us inner peace

Spiritual Benefits of Yoga

- Balances the Ida and Pingala *nadis*
- Brings awareness to the chakras
- Brings awareness to the Spirit
- Stimulates the energy centres
- Awakens the chakras
- Releases trapped energy in the body
- Increases our psychic abilities
- Improves the flow of *prana* in the body
- Brings us closer to the divine or God
- Cleanses and purifies the chakras
- Awakens Kundalini energy

Sun Salutation or *Surya Namaskar*

The Sun Salutation is the ultimate *asana*. It works on your whole body, is easy to execute and you can quickly see the results of this sequence on all levels: physical, mental and emotional. Do it a few times when you get up in the morning to help relieve stiffness and invigorate the body. This routine can help you stay grounded and heart-centred. The Sun Salutation covers all groups of muscles and organs, and when you perform it you are not only energizing your body, but are also getting a great workout to tone, oxygenate and strengthen mind, body and soul.

Because this pose works on your entire body – all the muscles, bones, organs, glands and systems – it works on all the chakras too. With just few rounds of Sun Salutations, your body will create heat quite quickly. Sun Salutation activates the *agni* (Fire) element and this will shoot an influx of energy to the rest of the body and chakras, opening them and getting them ready to release old energy and absorb new energy. After few rounds of Sun Salutations you will feel energized, rejuvenated and balanced. There are gurus in India who only practise Sun Salutations as their physical practice. This pose does it all!

If you are not feeling very confident yet in practising *asanas*, the Sun Salutations is definitely a good place to start. Doing eight to ten rounds in the morning can work wonders and slowly it will build strength and flexibility in your body.

1. Stand with your feet together at the top of the mat, hands beside your body in Tadasana or Mountain Pose. Inhale, exhale, then join both palms together in front of your chest (Pranamasana).

2. Inhale deeply, while slowly raising your hands over your head. Then gently take an arch back as far as possible (Hasta Uttanasana), while tightening your buttocks. Hold for 3 seconds.

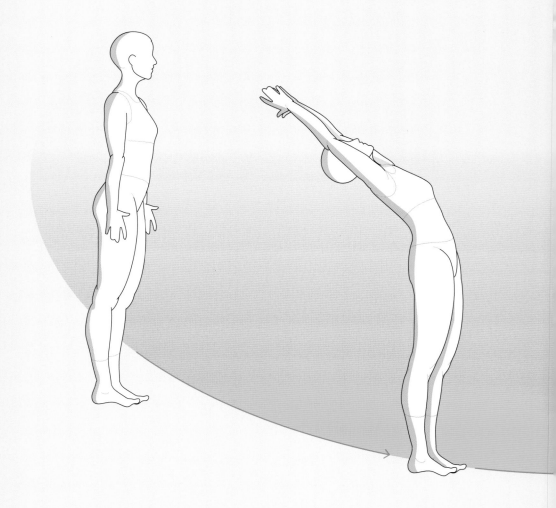

3. Slowly exhale and bend forward,
    keeping your knees straight,
    until your fingers touch the
    ground (if you can't touch the
    floor, go as close as you can).
    Bring your head in toward your
    knees (Padhastasana).

4. Slowly inhale and bring your right
    leg back (in a lunge position). The
    left leg is at a 90-degree angle (knee
    over ankle). Now look up as high as
    possible, arching your back (Ashwa
    Sanchalanasana). Put your hands on
    the ground.

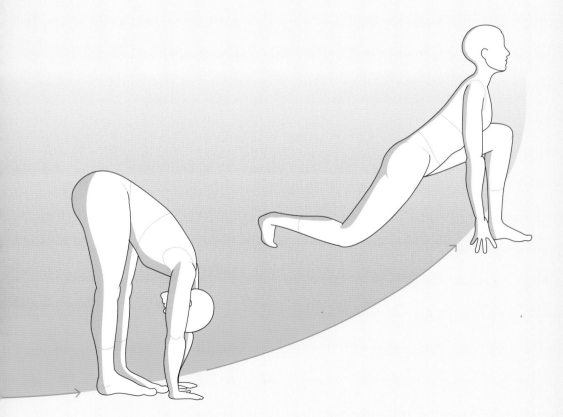

5. Exhale and slide your left foot back until it is beside the right one. With your weight supported on your palms and toes, straighten both legs so that your body forms a flat plane. Make sure your stomach is pulled in (Parvatasana).

6. Continue exhaling, then hold your breath and bend both knees to the floor. Place your chest and chin on the floor, then lower your chest and forehead to the floor (Ashtanga Namashkarasana or Eight Limbs Pose).

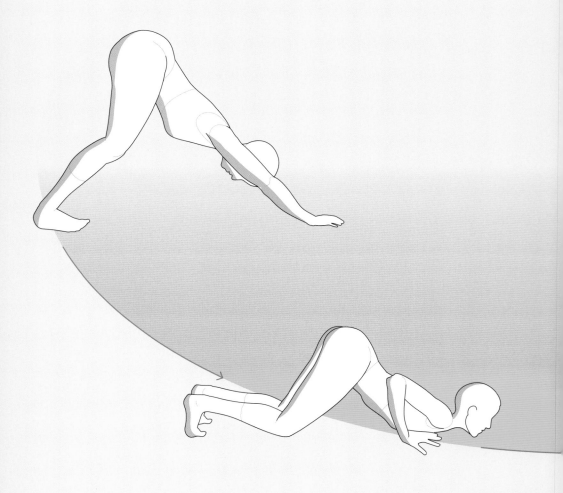

7. Flatten your feet, drop your buttocks down, then inhale and rise up into Cobra Pose (Bhujangasana). Stay here for 3 seconds.

8. Tuck your toes, lift your legs, exhale slowly and raise your hips until your feet and palms are flat on the floor and your arms and legs are straight in an inverted V position (Parvatasana).

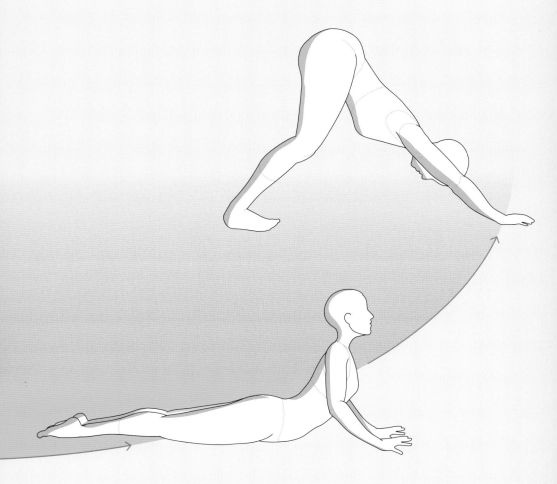

9. Inhale slowly and bring your right foot forward. It should be flat on the floor between your fingertips. The left leg should be almost straight behind you, with the knee on the floor. Raise your head, look up and arch your back (Ashwa Sanchalanasana).

10. Slowly exhale and bring your left foot forward next to your right one. Straighten your legs and stand, trying to keep your fingertips on the floor. Then try to touch your head to your knees (Padhastasana).

11. Slowly inhale, raise your arms and stretch back, as in Step 2 (see page 242). Don't forget to tighten your buttocks. Hold for 3 seconds.

12. Slowly exhale, lowering your arms to your sides or placing them in th Prayer Position. Relax.

13. Repeat on the other side. You can start by doing five of these poses, increasing to eight, and so on. And your speed can get quicker. The most important thing is to combine your breathing with each movement that you do.

Yoga Poses for the Chakras

In this section you will find explained two of the most common and popular poses for each chakras, making a total of 14 yoga poses. This will hopefully help you get started as you embark on your wonderful chakra-healing journey. As you gain more strength and confidence, feel free to explore other yoga poses (always under professional supervision, and being mindful of your own physical restrictions). Yoga poses are there to alleviate physical discomfort and emotional pain, not to cause further pain and discomfort.

All yoga poses stimulate and work on specific chakras, or on more than one chakra at the time. A good way to bring more chakra awareness into your practice is trying to feel the sensations in a particular chakra both during and after your yoga pose. Check how you felt performing the *asana*? Did you feel emotional? Did you feel strong? Did you feel more confident? In which part of your body did you feel the pose?

Pose for Muladhara: Tree Pose

This is a traditional Hatha yoga pose to stimulate concentration and balance. When you feel a bit off-balance emotionally and mentally, this pose can be a great help, because the physical body is also out of balance. This balancing pose calms your nervous system, is very good for relieving stress and grounding you, and offers mental balance. It also strengthens the legs and lower organs.

Tree Pose is all about being rooted and grounded on the yoga mat and in life. This pose invites you to stay firmly grounded and strong, just like a tree. Spread your roots deep down into the Earth, so that no matter how stormy everything around you is, you are still standing strong. Muladhara is our foundation and root chakra; it is the energy centre of balance and feeling grounded. Practising this pose regularly, or when you feel a bit out of sorts, can help you feel grounded and rooted.

Stage 1

1. Stand with both feet together on your mat. Make sure the whole soles of your feet touch the ground, and spread your toes. Stand firmly and engage your legs, roll your shoulders back, suck in your belly, lift your chest and place your arms next to your body. Have your chin parallel to the ground. Look forward.

2. Switch your body weight to the left leg. Inhale and bring your right foot to your left ankle. Exhale.

3. Inhale and join your palms together in front of your chest in the Prayer Position. Stay here for a count of five. Deeply inhale and exhale.

4. If this is too easy for you, inhale and raise both hands above your head, palms together.

5. Repeat on the other leg.

Stage 2

1. Start in the same position. Then inhale, bring your right foot up and place it on your left inner thigh. Push your left knee back, opening the left hip. Keep your right leg straight and strong.

2. Inhale and bring your hands above your head, palms together. Exhale. Stay there for few counts.

3. Slowly bring your leg down.

4. Repeat on the other leg.

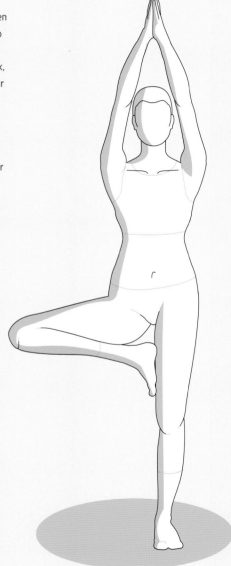

Pose for Muladhara: Savasana (Corpse Pose)

This is a traditional Hatha yoga pose and is often used for relaxation at the end of yoga practice involving *asanas*. Most people skip this part, but this pose is equally important as it integrates the energy and benefits of your practice into the organs, muscles and systems in your body. It also allows your physical body to relax after the practice and return to a normal rate. This *asana* is also great for grounding, because several points in your body make real contact with the ground beneath you, such as your heels, the back of your hands, the back of your head and your coccyx, making you feel supported. Whenever you feel out of your body or worried, are thinking too much and living in your head, come to this pose.

Corpse Pose is perfect for relaxing the nervous system after physical activity. Lying down on the floor, you are in contact with the ground that supports you, so you feel held and supported. It gives you a good feeling of integration with Muladhara's Earth energies. It is one of those yoga poses that reassures you that everything will be okay.

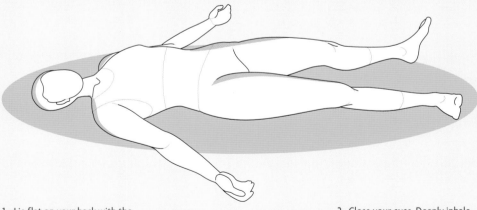

1. Lie flat on your back with the legs wide apart. Your arms should be beside you, away from your body, with the palms facing up and the shoulders touching the floor.

2. Close your eyes. Deeply inhale and exhale. Feel totally relaxed. Stay here for 10 minutes.

Pose for Svadhisthana: Goddess Pose

This is one of the favourite poses for grounding, empowering and activating the base energy centres. It opens the hips and chest while strengthening and toning the lower body. While practising this pose, you will feel more confident and powerful almost immediately. Goddess Pose screams Svadhisthana chakra. It is a hip-opening pose that will challenge your muscles and mind. When practising this *asana* you feel powerful and fierce. The focus is on the sacral plexus and the hips. It stimulates and activates Svadhisthana and all the organs related to it.

1. Start at the top of your mat in Tadasana or Mountain Pose (see page 242).

2. Step your left foot back about 1.2m (4ft) and turn your body, facing the long edge of your mat. Turn your toes 45 degrees so that they are facing outward. Bend your knees until your thighs are parallel to the floor. Get as low as you can, while keeping perfect alignment in your body. Make sure your knees are above your ankles. Draw your shoulder blades back and lift your chest. Make sure you are not leaning forward and that your torso is above your hips.

3. Bring your hands into the Prayer Position in front of your chest; alternatively you can bring them above your head. Deeply inhale and exhale.

4. Bring your awareness to Svadhisthana.

Pose for Svadhisthana: Extended Child's Pose

This is a resting pose that offers wonderful benefits. It is a more advanced pose than the usual Child's Pose because you open your legs wider, and so the stretch is deeper. It relieves pressure on the spine and lower back. It gently stretches the back, hips, thighs and ankles. It calms the mind, relieves stress and brings fresh blood to the brain. The focus of Extended Child's Pose is on your lower back and hips, and this is the area of the body that Svadhisthana oversees and controls. By practising this pose you stimulate the organs related to this area, releasing emotional stagnation and physical pain, and it relieves any tension in the body. When you release energy blockages in this chakra, you are unlocking the creative potential within you.

1. Begin by aligning your body on all fours: start by kneeling in a tabletop position, with the shoulders above the wrists, the palms firmly on the mat, the fingers wide open and the legs shoulder-width apart.

2. Extend your spine and walk your hands forward a little bit. Bring your toes together, pointing at each other. Bring your legs apart to the width of the yoga mat. Inhale through your nose and look forward.

3. Exhale and push back, so that your buttocks touch your heels.

4. Look forward and sink nicely onto the mat, touching your forehead to it. Extend your arms and bring your chest to the mat.

5. Stay here for a few deep inhalations and deep exhalations.

Pose for Manipura: Wheel Pose

This *asana* strengthens the spine and stretches the whole body. It is an invigorating backbend. It requires a lot of determination and inner power to push your body up and form an arch. In Sanskrit this pose is called Chakrasana, because it works on all chakras at once; and it copies the arch of the rainbow, which has the seven colours of the chakras. It offers a great deal of front-body stretch: from Muladhara to Vishuddha, the whole body is stretched and in alignment. It also helps to tone the muscles in the back and the calves. The introductory pose for this *asana* is the Bridge Pose.

1. Lie down on your back. Bend both knees and bring your feet close to your buttocks. Have your arms extended next to your body, and try to touch your heels with your middle fingers. Make sure your feet are straight and not pointing out. Have your legs open and hip-width apart.

2. Bend your arms and elbows and place your hands next to your ears, in a perpendicular way. Check once again that you are in perfect alignment.

3. Take a deep inhale and push yourself halfway up – your arms should be still bent and the top of your head touching the floor. Stay here for a count of five.

4. Release. Practise this Bridge Pose until you have sufficient strength in your arms to lift your up whole body.

5. Once you feel ready to go all the way up, take a deep inhale and lift your body up, staying in the Wheel Pose for a few breaths.

6. To come out of the pose, come down slowly to the mat.

7. After each round bring your knees to your chest and hug them for few breaths. This will alleviate the pressure in your back.

Pose for Manipura: Boat Pose

This core pose is yoga's original core work. This *asana* tones and strengthens your abdominal muscles, improves balance, stretches your hamstrings and improves digestion. It works in your hips flexors. This pose makes you feel confident as you work on Manipura.

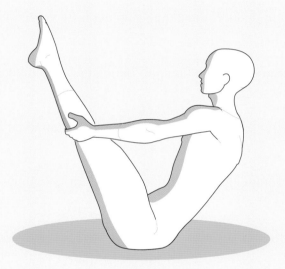

1. Begin seated on the floor. Bend your legs, with your feet on the floor, and roll your shoulders back. Lift your chest up. Make sure your back is nice and straight. Look forward.

2. Lean back slightly, keeping your back straight and the shoulder blades lifted. Place your hands under your calves or thighs. Inhale and lift your legs straight up.

3. Hold the pose and keep breathing for a count of five. Then release.

4. Repeat two more times.

Pose for Anahata: Camel Pose

This backbend stretches the entire front of the body: the ankles, thighs, groin, spine and shoulders. It is a chest-opener and works on the Manipura, Anahata and Vishuddha chakras. This pose keeps the spine flexible and healthy and can alleviate sciatica. It improves the digestion and massages the organs in this region. It also strengthens the respiratory system.

Any chest-opening yoga *asana* stimulates and balances Anahata. The spiritual meaning behind Camel Pose is that it not only encourages you to open your chest physically to stimulate the organs involved, but also asks you to open your heart. When you execute this *asana* your focus is on your heart centre and feeling the love within.

1. Start by kneeling on the floor without sitting on your heels, so that your body weight is supported by your knees. Make sure that your knees and feet are straight and are separated by the same width as your hips. Place your palms on your lower back so that your fingers are facing down.

2. Inhale and slowly lean backward, gradually pushing your hips forward. Go as far as you can, keeping your thighs straight. You can stay here, taking deep inhalations and exhalations.

3. If you can go further back, try to grab your heels. Tuck your toes to make this a bit easier.

4. Once in the pose, keep pushing your hips forward, opening your chest and dropping your head backward. Do this for few breaths.

5. To come out of the pose, inhale and slowly come forward.

6. Exhale and go into Child's Pose (see page 253).

7. Repeat for two more rounds.

Pose for Anahata: Cobra Pose

This *asana* is part of the Sun Salutation sequence (see page 241). It increases flexibility in the spine and can alleviate back pain, lumbago, sciatica and other back problems. It tones the heart and alleviates neck pain. It also increases blood circulation.

Cobra Pose brings more awareness to Anahata and awakens spiritual aspirations. It also increases lung capacity, bring benefits to the abdominal organs and relieves constipation.

1. Lie on your belly, facing down on the mat. Place your palms on the floor under the shoulders. Keep the legs extended and the feet together. Spread your fingers wide while pressing the pelvis, thighs and top of the feet firmly into the floor.

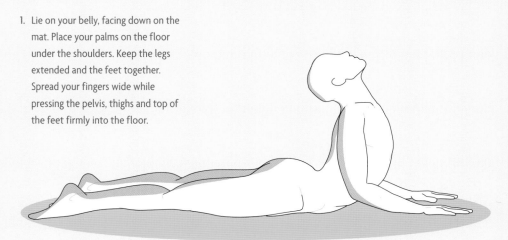

2. Inhale and slowly bring your torso up, pressing the palms on the floor. Lift your chest up and roll your shoulders back. If you have a stiff back, try an easier variation first, where the elbows and the forearms are kept on the floor: think of a sphinx pose. The arms are perpendicular to the floor and as close as possible to your sides.

3. Look up and stretch your neck. If you can, stretch your arms straight and go all the way up, making sure that you don't put any strain on the neck or shrink the shoulders. This is a heart-opening pose, so this region is exposed.

4. Drop your head backward. Inhale and exhale for five rounds.

5. To come out of the pose, tuck your toes, inhale and exhale, then push your buttocks back and go into Child's Pose (see page 253).

6. Repeat for two more rounds.

Pose for Vishuddha: Fish Pose

This backbend is a traditional Hatha stretching and opening yoga pose. It works on all the major chakras from Muladhara to Sahasrara. It stretches the throat, chest, abdomen, hip flexors and intercostal muscles, and strengthens the back and neck. It encourages better breathing and helps to relieve spinal tension and improve posture. This is a great *asana* to practise after a long day in front of your computer.

As Fish Pose stretches the throat, where Vishuddha is, it activates and stimulates this energy centre. With this *asana* we are stretching the vocal cords, an important element in expressing ourselves and communicating. This pose also dissolves trapped energy in the throat.

1. Lie down on your back, with your knees bent and the soles of your feet flat on your mat. Lift your hips and place your hands facing down, beneath your buttocks. Bring your forearms and elbows close to your body.

2. On the inhale, bend your elbows and press firmly into your forearms and elbows, lifting your chest and head from the floor. Gently find the natural curve of your spine.

3. Push your shoulder blades back and lift your chest higher toward the ceiling, elongating your spine. Stretch your neck and slowly place the crown of your head on the floor. If your head cannot reach the floor, place a rolled-up blanket or cushion underneath it.

4. If it feels comfortable, you can stretch your legs and point your toes. Release your hands from under your pelvis and place them next to your body, with slightly bent elbows, pushing up your body with the forearms.

5. Bring your awareness to Vishuddha. Stay here for five breaths.

6. Repeat two more times.

Pose for Vishuddha: Cat/Cow with Lion's Breath

Cat/Cow stretches are some of my favourite yoga poses and I always include them in my practice – they are wonderful preparation for any *asana* class. They offer total spinal movement and a warm-up to the upper body, creating good space and articulation along the joints and vertebrae. They relieve tension and stress in your face, jaw and tongue. On the spiritual level, this is a great pose to clear Vishuddha of any energy blockages.

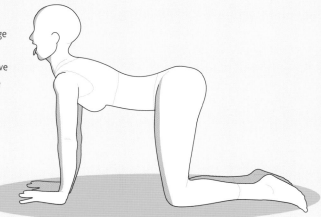

1. Come to a tabletop position (see page 253) and place your legs hip-width apart. Your shoulders should be above your wrists. Make sure there is a nice alignment from the tailbone to the head. Spread your fingers wide.

2. Start with a deep inhalation through your nose. As you inhale, lift your tail, drop your belly and look up.

3. As you exhale through your nose, tuck your tail in, arch your back, suck in your belly and drop your head and gaze to your navel. Be mindful when practising this *asana*, and move with your breath.

4. Keep doing this for few more rounds. Create a nice rhythm with the inhalation and exhalation.

5. After a few rounds, begin to introduce Lion's Breath on your exhalations. Inhale through your nose in Cow Pose as usual, but on the exhalation open your mouth and make an "Ahhhh" sound from your throat, sticking your tongue out.

6. Continue doing this for a count of ten.

7. When you finish, inhale deeply and, on the exhale, come into Child's Pose (see page 253) and rest for a count of five.

8. Repeat two more rounds

Pose for Ajna: Chair Pose

Chair Pose is an essential part of the Sun Salutation, but it can also be practised on its own. This *asana* strengthens the thighs and feet muscles. It tones your abdominal muscles, buttocks and the entire body, and stretches your shoulders. It increases the heart rate, stimulating the circulatory system. This standing pose stimulates your digestive system and generates body heat.

The focus of this pose is on the upper body, the head and the eyes. Ajna is associated with the pineal and pituitary glands, which produce hormones in our body. By practising Chair Pose you stimulate these glands, and it not only helps you to balance Ajna chakra, but also to balance life.

1. Stand at the top of your mat in Tadasana or Mountain Pose (see page 242). Bring your feet together with the big toes touching, and spread your toes. Stand firmly on the ground.

2. Inhale and raise your arms above your head, with the palms facing each other. Stretch your torso up.

3. Exhale and bend your knees, bringing your thighs parallel to the floor, as low as you can. Draw your tailbone down. Your knees should be touching each other and projecting slightly over your feet.

4. Lengthen your body, stretch your arms, look up and breathe. Shift your weight down to your heels. (If you are having trouble balancing or finding it difficult to get down, try opening your legs hip-width apart. And instead of having your arms above your head, place them in front of you, for more control and support.) With each exhalation, try to get lower if you can. Breath for a count of five.

5. Inhale and slowly come back up to Tadasana.

Pose for Ajna: Thunderbolt Pose

This is a traditional and ancient seated yoga pose that is often used in meditation and breathing exercises. It stretches the thighs, ankles and knees, improves posture, strengthens the back and stimulates the digestive system. Regular practice of this *asana* can release stress and bring calmness to the mind. It also opens the chest and shoulders. This pose can release neck and back pain associated with sedentary desk jobs.

Thunderbolt Pose helps to align Ajna because it encourages you to observe your thoughts and mind. Observing our thoughts and not engaging with them is a way to detach and not get involved in negative thoughts.

1. Start in a high kneeling position on your mat, with the feet and legs together.

2. Sit on your heels, with the toes pointing straight back. Sit nice and tall. Make sure that your back makes a straight line from the tailbone to the crown of the head. Roll your shoulders back and lift your chest slightly. Suck in your belly, so that it supports your back and holds the posture. Place your hands on the floor or on your thighs, with the palms facing down. (If sitting back isn't comfortable for you, try placing a blanket or cushion under your feet. You can also use the support of a block or cushion between your feet and your buttocks until you develop more stretch in your ankles and thighs.)

3. Take deep inhalations and exhalations. Observe your breath. Close your eyes and bring your awareness to Ajna. Stay here for 3–5 minutes.

Pose for Sahasrara: Half Moon Pose

This is traditional Hatha yoga pose that can be a little challenging at first. It requires balance, coordination and core strength. It strengthens the abdomen, ankles, thighs, buttocks and back, as well as the groin, hamstrings, chest and spine. This *asana* helps to release stress and aids concentration. Half Moon Pose stimulates the energy of Sahasrara as it puts pressure on the head. It helps to relieve stress and improve coordination and balance.

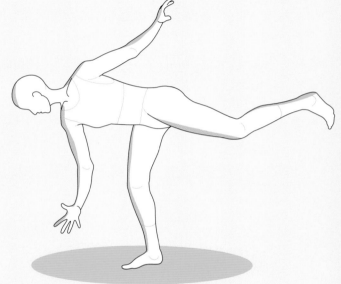

1. Stand in the middle of your mat with your feet together and your hands on your waist. Inhale and jump, opening your legs wider than hip-distance apart.

2. Exhale and turn your right foot sideways toward the top of your mat.

3. Inhale and extend your arms out to the sides.

4. Exhale and slowly bring your right hand next to your right foot, while simultaneously lifting your left leg parallel to the floor. Raise your left arm 90 degrees so that it is aligned with the left shoulder. Keep your left foot engage and flexed.

5. Once you reach the right foot with your right hand, inhale, open your chest and look up toward your left hand. (If you are finding difficult to reach the floor, use a prop or block to create some height. As you keep practising you will eventually reach the floor with ease.) Take five breaths here.

6. Repeat on the other side.

Pose for Sahasrara: Half Lotus Pose

This is a beginner's version of the Lotus Pose and can prepare you for the full *asana*.
It is suitable for people who have less flexibility or body restrictions in the lower
body. This pose is generally used during meditation and breathing exercises. It is
good for opening the hips, and it stretches the knees and ankles. It also encourages
good posture and eases pressure in the back.

Half Lotus is the pose that is generally used for meditation, while full Lotus Pose is
the *asana* yogis usually do when meditating. Lord Shiva and Buddha adopted this
seated pose, so it is considered to act as a gateway to higher consciousness and
connects you with cosmic energies through Sahasrara.

1. Start in a crossed-legs position.

2. With both hands, gently lift the
    right foot and place it on the
    left thigh, close to the hip or
    groin, with the sole of the foot
    facing upward. Adjust your foot
    so that it is as high as possible
    on your right thigh. Make any
    necessary adjustment with
    the other foot so that it feels
    comfortable and there is no
    strain on your ankles or knees.
    Sit straight, with your back nice
    and tall and your chest raised.

3. Inhale and bring both hands in
    front of your chest in Namaste
    or Prayer Position. Close your
    eyes. Bring your attention to
    Sahasrara. Breathe deeply in and
    out of the navel centre.

4. Repeat with the other leg.
    One side will probably feel
    easier than the other – that's
    absolutely normal. Make sure
    you do both sides for an equal
    length of time.

"Choose to focus your energy on bringing balance into your mind, body and soul. Regular yoga practice will help you to be your highest and best self while balancing the chakras."

Traditional Kundalini Tantra

In Sanskrit, *Kundalini* means "coiled snake" and this is why Kundalini is represented as a snake. It is the sleeping, dormant energy located at Muladhara, and it is believed that this energy is responsible for forming physical new life in the mother's uterus. Once the baby has been formed, the energy coils up and sits dormant at Muladhara, waiting to be awakened. This is of great potential and power, and is also known as the divine feminine energy Shakti, which according to Hinduism should be awakened and rise up to join the masculine energy Shiva, located at Sahasrara.

So Kundalini yoga is the practice of Tantric techniques that are used in a systematic way to awaken Kundalini energy. Kundalini yoga uses *asanas*, mantras, breathing techniques, *mudras* and *kriyas*. The regular practice of Kundalini yoga prepares the mind, body and soul for the awakening of the creative energy of Shakti.

You should clean and awaken the chakras first, before attempting to awaken Kundalini. Bringing balance into the chakras and the Ida and Pingala *nadis* through regular yoga practice prepares the body, and Kundalini therefore rises from Muladhara through the spine (Sushumna *nadi*) up to Sahasrara.

All the exercises shared in this book are part of my own daily yoga practice, focusing on the chakra system.

Practice for Muladhara: *Moola Bandha* (root lock)

This *bandha*, or body lock, unlocks Muladhara energy. It purifies this chakra and awakens the Kundalini *shakti* that is dormant there. It also strengthens the pelvic floor, calms the nervous system and relaxes the mind. When practising *bandhas* you are locking the energy in, therefore there is a boost of *prana* in that area. In Muladhara the energy is *apana* (the energy of purification, elimination and detoxification) and having a boost of this energy will unlock Muladhara energy because it cleanses and releases.

Duration: 3–5 rounds

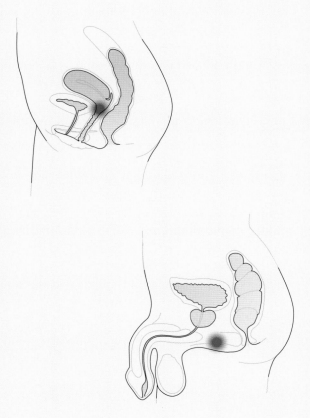

1. Sit cross-legged on the floor.

1. Feel the pressure in the region of Muladhara, and bring your awareness to this point.

2. Inhale deeply through your nose. Hold your breath and apply the *bandha* by squeezing the perineum, which is Muladhara's trigger point. Hold it for as long as you can. Then release it.

3. Next, start contracting and releasing the Moola *bandha* rhythmically and in a synchronized fashion, at the rate of one contraction per second. Do this for 1 minute.

4. Repeat the practice two more times.

Practice for Svadhisthana: HAR Mantra

This practice can be done after your yoga practice or meditation. It clears the emotional blockages in the area of Svadhisthana, releases tension and negative energy, and on some occasions can release physical pain. By chanting "HAR" you are also creating space for creative energy, bringing you great prosperity and abundance. Every time I do this practice I feel lighter in my lower abdomen and more flexible. I totally love this mantra, which is very powerful, and the experience you get by repeating it is quite profound.

Duration: 5–8 minutes

1. Stand with your legs hip-width apart. Bring your hands above Svadhisthana – you can make the shape of a downward-pointing triangle. Close your eyes.

2. Bring your awareness to this chakra. Take a deep inhalation through your nose, and on the exhalation, chant from Svadhisthana, pulling your belly in with each sound of the mantra "HAR HAR HAR HAR HAR"... repeated non-stop. This has to be done very powerfully and loud enough that you can feel the vibration of the mantra in this area of your body. Remember to pull in your belly when saying "HAR" and, as you get in rhythm, chant faster.

3. Keep chanting continuously for at least 2 or 3 minutes.

4. When you finish, take a deep inhale through your nose and, as you exhale, bend forward. Keep breathing in through your nose and out through your mouth. Relax in this pose for few breaths.

5. Repeat the sequence two more times.

6. At the end of your practice, lie down on your back in Savasana (Corpse Pose) for 5–10 minutes.

Practice for Manipura: *Uddiyana Bandha* (abdominal lock)

This *bandha* cleanses Manipura and activates the energy of this chakra. It stimulates the digestive organs and massage the abdominal organs. It is great for giving yourself a good boost of energy in the mornings.

Duration: 3–5 rounds

1. On an empty stomach, stand with your legs shoulder-width apart. Bend your knees a little and lean forward slightly. Press your palms onto your knees. Exhale completely.

2. Now contract the abdominal muscles as far as possible, both inward and upward. Hold your breath for few counts.

3. Release and breathe normally.

4. Repeat the sequence two more times.

Practice for Anahata: *Ajapa Japa* Meditation ("So Hum" meditation)

This mantra meditation helps us to discover our inner self and gives us clarity of mind. It helps us identify and connect with the universal energy. The idea of being one with the universe and constantly supported gives us a feeling of protection, belonging and unconditional love. When you are seeking support, love and protection, the "So Hum" mantra (which means "I Am That") can offer you just that. This meditation holds the vibration of love and the universe and therefore benefits Anahata. It relieves stress, anxiety and anger. It brings the divine within you. It opens your heart to compassion, forgiveness and gratitude.

Duration: 10 minutes

1. Sitting in a comfortable position, bring your awareness to your breath.

SO   HUM

2. On the inhale, mentally say "SO".

3. On the exhale, mentally say "HUM".

4. Continue in this manner until you create a nice rhythm between your breathing and the mantra, keeping a constant awareness of the mantra and its meaning.

Practice for Vishuddha: *Jalandhara Bandha* (chin/throat lock)

This *bandha* clears Vishuddha by removing energy blockages, enabling better communication and self-expression. The stimulus on the throat helps to balance thyroid function, promoting good health in this gland. It also helps to relieve stress and anxiety.

Duration: 3–5 rounds

1. Sit in a meditative position. Place the palms of the hands on your knees, applying Jnana *mudra* (see page 235). Inhale so that your lungs are about two-thirds full, and hold your breath. Drop your chin down closer to your chest, making a double chin. Lift your chest and lengthen your torso. Drop your shoulders away from your ears.

2. Hold the breath for as long as is comfortable. (For beginners, this will be only few seconds of breath retention. With practice, you will be able to hold the breath longer.)

3. Lift your chin up and finish your inhalation before releasing the breath.

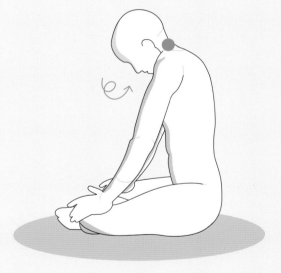

Practice for Ajna: *Nadi Shodhana* (alternate-nostril breathing)

This *pranayama* breath-control practice stimulates Ajna, improves concentration and balances the breath and the hemispheres of the brain. It also balances the Ida and Pingala *nadis*. It lowers blood pressure, reduces stress and relieves tension and anxiety. It detoxifies and cleanses.

Caution: Do not perform this *pranayama* with a blocked nose, a cold or a fever. Start from Stage 1 and do not strain your breathing.

Duration: 10–15 minutes

Stage 1: beginner's technique

1. Sit comfortably in any meditative *asana*, making sure that your spine is nice and straight. Take a moment to relax your mind and body. Relax your shoulders.

2. Start by taking deep inhalations and exhalations. Close your eyes. Make a Jnana *mudra* (see page 235), with your left hand resting on your left knee. With your right hand make the Nasagra *mudra* (index and middle finger on Ajna between the eyebrows), with the thumb above your right nostril and the ring finger above your left nostril.

3. Close the right nostril with the thumb. Inhale and exhale through the left nostril five times. The inhalation and exhalation should be normal and effortless (you are using the thumb and ring finger in turn to block and unblock the flow of air through the nostrils).

4. After completing five breaths, release the right nostril and press the left nostril with the ring finger, blocking the flow of air. Inhale and exhale through the right nostril five times, keeping the breathing normal.

5. Lower the hand and breathe five times through both nostrils, as normal. This represents one round.

6. Do five rounds of this alternate-nostril breathing. Make sure you master this sequence before moving on to Stage 2 (see page 274).

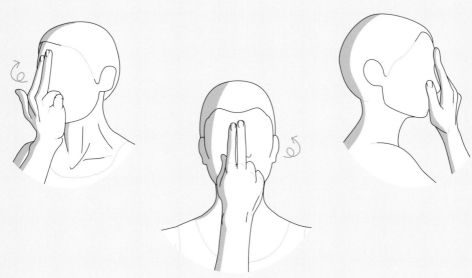

Stage 2: intermediate technique

1. Sitting in the same position, count the length of the inhalation and exhalation through the left nostril, right nostril and both nostrils. While inhaling, mentally count "one, two, three" comfortably. While exhaling, mentally count "one, two, three". The inhalation and exhalation should be equal.

2. Practise for five rounds until you master this sequence and you can eventually count to ten instead of three. Then you can move on to the more advanced technique in Stage 3.

Stage 3: advanced technique

1. In this technique the basic pattern of alternate-nostril breathing is established as 1:1. So breathe in through the left nostril and count "one, two, three", then close the left nostril and breathe out "one, two, three" through the right nostril.

2. Inhale through the right nostril and count "one, two, three", then close the right nostril and exhale through the left nostril, counting "one, two, three". This represents one round.

3. Continue for five to ten rounds.

4. Release and breathe normally.

5. After a week of doing this, if you are experiencing no difficulties, increase the length of the inhalation and exhalation by one. Continue practising until this sequence is done without any strain and feels comfortable, and the count reaches 10:10.

Practice for Bindu Visarga: *Bhramari Pranayama* (humming-bee breath)

Bhramari pranayama is a very calming and soothing breathing exercise that quickly induces a meditative state. The humming sound calms and relaxes the nervous system. It brings clarity of mind and reduces stress. This breathing exercise also stimulates the physical senses, promotes mental strength and speech. It is recommended for people who normally suffer from headaches and migraines, although it should not be practised while experiencing a headache. This exercise works on Vishuddha, Ajna, Sahasrara and Bindu Visarga chakras. It clears and stimulates them through the vibration and frequency of the sound.

Duration: 5 minutes

1. Sit in a comfortable meditation position, with the hands resting in Jnana *mudra* (see page 235). Close your eyes. Relax your mind and body. Keep your lips gently closed, with the teeth slightly separated.

2. Use your index or middle fingers to cover your ears by pressing on your ear flaps, but not by inserting your fingers inside your ears. Bring your attention to Ajna. Keep your body still. Inhale through your nose.

3. Exhale slowly while making a steady humming sound like a bee. Continue for the duration of the exhalation. The humming sound should be smooth. Make the sound until the end of the exhalation and then repeat five times.

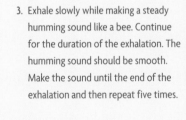

"By tapping into the Kundalini flow, I unfold the beauty, power and manifestation energies within me. I am a creative expression of the universe and Kundalini amplifies this."

Positive Affirmations

It is proven that positive affirmations – statements of truth that you aspire to attain – help to reprogramme the mind. When you repeat an affirmation over and over again, the subconscious picks up on it as the present reality. Does this mean that people have the ability to turn around their lives as they know them? In one word: yes.

You can co-create your world to your own specifications. Want a better relationship? Start by telling yourself that you deserve it. Once you have heard this for so long, your mind will not settle for anything else. Want a better job? Learn to recite affirmations about your passions, and watch how many doors open in your direction.

I regularly hear people saying that repeating positive affirmations won't make them lose weight, get the dream job they wish for or find them the right partner, and so on. I have heard all the negative comments regarding practising positive affirmations. But this is the thing: if you are practising positive affirmations day and night, saying them from your heart and not from your mouth – and by this I mean saying them with conviction and true intention – then there is a shift of energy, and that positive shift in your mindset opens up a world of endless possibilities and abundance to you.

I totally get it when people say that positive affirmations "didn't work" for them, because it's quite likely that the reason why they didn't work is because they weren't executed properly and for a long period of time. People often expect changes to happen right away. If we don't see results immediately, we give up and move on to the next thing. We generally operate this way and live our lives rushing from one idea to another, without actually processing what is involved. We are accustomed to this way of living and lack patience, and this is why many people try shortcuts in everything they do – focusing only on the final result and forgetting that the actual journey and experience of the process are what have real value.

The Power of Words and Feelings

Another important aspect regarding positive affirmations is that we tend to forget about the power of words. Let me break this down so that you can understand better what I mean. Words are a form of sound, and sounds create vibration, and there is a certain frequency within that sound. Now the words itself aren't powerful – what makes this sound powerful is the intention behind it.

Words can be very empowering or destructive, as I'm sure you will agree. The intention behind those words will raise or lower their vibrational frequency. When "I love you" is said with truth, it is healing, empowering and felt in each and every cell of our bodies. And if someone says, " I hate you" with a strong negative energy behind it, you will feel that, too. Songs for little children are very soothing; poems can be empowering and inspiring; and so are positive affirmations. They are made up of words, and you are the one who adds the intention behind those words.

Another example taken from daily life concerns the way in which parents or carers bring up children. If you raise a child in a loving, positive, encouraging environment, where he's constantly told positive words, then it is more likely that the child will be a confident individual in the future; whereas if you raise a child in a hostile, abusive and unloving environment, then it is more likely that he will be an individual with a lack of confidence who experiences traumas.

Words are attached to feelings, so you might not remember everything that was said at your birthday party when you turned eight years old, but you will probably remember an exciting or upsetting moment at your party (I hated clowns for some reason). Our mind is free to store as many happy or sad memories as it wishes. We don't store words much, but we do store the emotions and feelings that we felt when we heard those words; and, more specifically, we hold on to those feelings. They are in our subconscious and unconscious minds, and so when we are in similar situations, those emotions come to the fore and remind us how to react to them. This is how we create patterns in our lives, responding and interacting with the world and with experiences based on our self-beliefs and past experiences.

Sometimes we don't even know why we are feeling in a certain way toward something or someone. As an example, if you got scared of the clown at your birthday party when you were a little child, then there is a good chance that as an

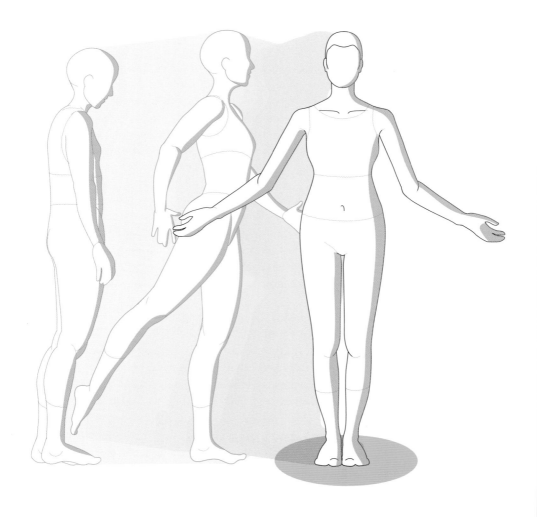

adult you won't like clowns or hire them for your children's birthday parties. Can you see the pattern now? You won't like clowns until you change the way you feel about them, by reversing the information stored in your subconscious mind. Do you want to free yourself from being scared of clowns? Probably not. It's really not relevant to your life now, unless you are suffering from nightmares and mental illness as a result.

My point is that whatever you think about yourself – whatever limiting self-beliefs you are holding on to, in a way that you feel you can't move forward in life and free yourself of them – you have the power to reverse this. It lies within you to let go of past emotions and be happy. Past experiences and traumas will not necessarily determine your future. It's all about changing bad habits and negative thoughts into positive ones.

Repetitive words, statements and phrases can either make you or destroy you. Be mindful with the type of words you say to yourself and others, especially when you are repeating those words out loud and in your mind. They are a form of manifestation of the sound and can generate strong emotions.

In my classes I encourage people to become aware of the story or narrative they are telling themselves, because often we are not conscious of what we are telling ourselves throughout the day, and what we think about ourselves is based on past experiences – this is information that we retrieve from the subconscious or unconscious mind. We all have an inner critic that tells us we are not good enough, we are not worthy, we are too fat, too thin, we are stupid, we are unable to wish for better, and so on. We don't need to remember these words; what we should remember is the emotion attached to those words.

I am a firm believer of practising positive affirmations in the right way to reverse some of these limiting self-beliefs, bad habits and negative patterns. Positive affirmations can reprogramme the mind, and they must be said together with an emotion that is linked to it. You see, you have probably forgotten most of what was said on the day of your graduation, but you probably remember the emotion that you felt on that special day. Am I right? Research shows that 7 per cent of meaning is communicated through the spoken word, 38 per cent through tone of voice and 55 per cent through body language.

How to Use Positive Affirmations in an Effective Way

First, you must identify the issue you would like to change. Then choose one or two affirmations: the ones that resonate with you the most. Make sure you are committed to saying your positive affirmation for at least 40 days consecutively.

Attach a positive emotion to the affirmation. For example, a client of mine decided that she was going to use the "I am strong" affirmation when she was in the gym lifting weights and working out. You can also think of a beautiful memory and recall it while saying the affirmation. For example, if you say "I am happy, and I deserve to be happy", link it to moments in your life when you were very happy; by doing this repeatedly you are convincing yourself that you are indeed happy, you have lived that, have experienced it, and the proof is that you have beautiful memories of it.

When saying the affirmation first thing in the morning, visualize it and place your hands on your heart. Repeat the affirmation throughout the day. If something good happens to you on that day which you can relate to the positive affirmation you are saying, use that, as you are already manifesting it!

Trust the process, and believe that we are beings able to create and manifest what we want in our lives. Stick with it and don't give up. Most importantly, make sure your affirmation comes from a place of love and integrity.

Healing Affirmations for the Chakras

Chakra-healing affirmations are positive statements designed to tap into the energy of each chakra and recalibrate its vibration, bringing balance to the body. Our chakras come out of balance easily and frequently, and when the chakras are not aligned, this can manifest in a variety of emotions and in a negative way in our physical, mental and emotional bodies. So it is important to check in with ourselves regularly and understand what is going on internally.

Healing affirmations for the chakras use the power of words, which can have either good energy or bad energy. Unfortunately, words with bad energy can be also very powerful and are able to destroy us emotionally and mentally. I want to highlight here that I am not only referring to the words someone else says to us, but also the words we tell ourselves. Most people don't realize that a lot of the thoughts we have in our heads are directed at ourselves. We know this as our inner critic: that little voice, or inner self, that tells us we are not good enough, or we are too big or too thin... Those thoughts then become words, and the words become actions. The more you tell yourself (or someone else) that they are not good enough, the more that person will believe the statement and start behaving like that.

With chakra-healing affirmations we can reverse any negative thoughts/words that we tell ourselves. When saying a particular healing affirmation, we are tapping into the chakra in question and are sending the positive energy of the affirmation directly to that chakra, which will be stimulated and will release any energies that are not in alignment with it.

Muladhara

- I am ready to release all my fears
- I am safe and protected
- All my basic needs are fulfilled
- I live a life of abundance
- I love my body
- I am grounded and connected to Mother Earth
- I belong to this planet
- I am full of energy and vitality
- I feel safe and confident
- Everything is as it should be
- I am powerful, rooted and strong
- I am confident in everything I do
- Doors open and opportunities come easily to me
- I have what I need to create my dream life
- I am open to all possibilities
- I nurture my mind, body and soul every day
- I only choose and consume nurturing food

Svadhisthana

- I am connected with the divine within me
- I am a creative being
- I nurture my body with love and admiration
- I accept my sexuality
- I flow in life, and everything within me flows
- I am enough and I do enough
- I honour myself just the way I am
- I am a unique, beautiful being
- I live my life with passion
- Creativity flows within me
- It is my birthright to receive pleasure
- My body is the temple of my soul
- I honour and connect with my sacred space
- I accept and honour my emotions
- I express myself graciously
- I am worthy of love
- I enjoy pleasure in all areas of my life
- I am a sensual and desirable being

Manipura

- I accept myself and I feel positively empowered
- I am enough and I do enough
- I am strong
- I move forward in my life
- I live my life with purpose
- I am in touch with my feelings
- I am able to complete and achieve my goals in life
- I make my own decisions with confidence and conviction
- I use my power for good
- I am in control of my emotions
- I am full of life and good energy
- I am motivated to pursue my true purpose
- I am an achiever
- I release the need to control
- People around me value me as a person
- I have high self-esteem and know I am valuable
- I have a lot to offer to this world
- People trust me and see me as an inspiration
- I release myself from the past
- I succeed in everything I do

Anahata

- I love myself unconditionally
- I give and receive love fully and effortlessly
- I am able to forgive myself and others
- My heart is pure
- I forgive myself for my mistakes
- I forget those who hurt me
- I see compassion every day in my life
- My heart is full of love and gratitude
- My heart radiates love and kindness
- I release and let go of all resentment
- I am worthy of true and pure love
- I am loved
- I choose love every day
- I create loving and supporting relationships
- My heart is filled with joy and gratitude

Vishuddha

- I express myself with grace and integrity
- I communicate my ideas and desires effectively
- I express my emotions
- I speak my truth openly and freely
- I am honest and I attract what I deserve
- I listen to others with interest
- I am understood and heard
- My words empower people
- Everything I say comes from a place of love and integrity
- I am safe and trust others to let me express myself truthfully
- My voice is clear and powerful
- My words are peaceful
- I am confident about myself
- I am honest and authentic in my speech and actions
- I trust others

Ajna

- I am connected to my inner guidance
- I am connected to my Higher Self
- I open myself to energy and opportunities
- My life flows easily toward my purpose
- I trust the highest good is unfolding and blessing me
- I choose to tap into my inner guidance
- My third eye sees everything
- My third eye radiates wisdom
- I am guided in every step I take
- I see and manifest the life I want
- I live in alignment with my true self
- I am connected to the spiritual world
- I see the divine in everything and everyone
- I am wise and I trust my decisions
- My third eye is open and radiates indigo-blue light
- Every situation is an opportunity to grow
- I see my truth through Ajna chakra
- I see beyond the illusions
- My mind, body and Spirit are healed

Sahasrara

- I am a divine being
- I am part of this abundant universe
- Everything is good in my life
- I belong to the Earth and the universe
- I am connected to the universe
- The divine Source is my guide
- I trust the miracles of the universe
- I am connected to the divine light
- I am open to receive cosmic energy
- White light radiates from my Sahasrara chakra
- I am pure light and love
- I am whole and complete
- I am unity
- I am healed
- I am at peace with myself and others

- I honour the divine within me
- I cherish my Spirit
- I trust God
- I understand my life purpose
- I accept and receive pure love
- I am open to receive the divine light to flow through me
- My chakras are awakened and ready to receive divine energy

"My words are a powerful and pure manifestation of the positive energies in my body. I consciously choose to speak words that serve my soul purpose and empower others.

May the words I say serve my highest good."

Afterword

I hope that, after reading this book and putting into practice what you have learned in it, you can have the life of abundance and love that you deserve. I hope this book opens you up to a world of infinite possibilities, where you are able to manifest your dreams and live a more inspiring and meaningful life. Everything written here is based on my research, my self-studies and my personal experiences.

Chakras are present in every single corner of this beautiful world. You just need to open yourself up to see and feel them. I personally can't see our lives without chakras, can you?

References

Books

Kalwani, Rohan, *Kundalini Awakening, Rising and Yoga for Chakra Balancing: A Comprehensive Beginner's Guide to Yoga, Chakras, Kundalini, Meditation, Self-Healing and Therapeutic Techniques* (2016)

McGeough, Marion, *A Beginner's Guide to the Chakras* (CreateSpace Independent Publishing Platform, 2013)

Miller, Anama, *Aura Balancing: 13 Ways to Balance Your Aura* (2014)

Smith, Colin G, *Chakras for Beginners Guide Book* (2014)

Online

"The 7 Chakras", **Chakras Info**, www.chakras.info/7-chakras/

"A Beginner's Guide to the 7 Chakras and Their Meanings", **Healthline**, www.healthline.com/health/fitness-exercise/7-chakras

"The Seven Bodies of Human", **Nepal Yoga Home**, www.nepalyogahome.com/?s=seven+bodies

Samadhi Yoga Ashram (Kundalini Yoga TTC by Yogi Vishnu), www.samadhiyogaashram.com

"Kundalini and the Seven Bodies", **Satrakshita**, www.satrakshita.com/kundalini_and_the_seven_bodies.htm

World Peace Yoga School, www.worldpeaceyogaschool.com

Yoga Journal, www.yogajournal.com

Glossary

affirmation: A positive thinking or statement that, when repeated with conviction, brings emotional and mental support

agni: Fire

amrit: The nectar of immortality

asana: A body posture in yoga

Ascended Master: One of the enlightened spiritual beings who once habituated the Earth

astral body: The subtle body that is related to emotional experience

Atman: Spirit or soul

aura: Electromagnetic field

bandha: A body lock used in yoga practices

bija mantra: A one-syllable sound or word

bindu: Point or dot

Bindu Visarga: The chakra at the back of the head (literally, "falling on the drop")

Brahmin: An intellectual, teacher or priest who protects sacred learning down the generations

causal body: The cause or seed of the subtle body and physical body

chi: Life-force energy

cosmic body: The sixth subtle body of humans

deity: A god or goddess; a supreme being

dharma: Universal truth that makes life and the universe possible

energy body: A subtle body made of thousands of *nadis*, chakras and spiritual energy

etheric body: The first or lowest layer in the energy field of humans, also known as the emotional body.

guru: Teacher, guide or master

Hatha yoga: A classical form of yoga that involves a set of physical techniques, breathing and meditation

Higher Self: The eternal, conscious and intelligent being considered one's real self

karma: Action, work or deed; the spiritual principle of cause and effect

ki: Life-force energy

kosha: A layer that covers the Atman/soul

kriya: A completed action, technique or practice in yoga focused on achieving a specific goal

Kundalini: Coiled serpent; the divine feminine energy dormant at Muladhara

linga: Usually an abstract votary object that symbolizes the Hindu deity Shiva

Lower Self: The lower nature of the self, usually associated with bad behaviour

lower-triangle chakras: The three lower chakras located on the lower body: Muladhara (base of the spine), Svadhisthana (pelvis) and Manipura (navel)

manas shakti: Mental force

mandala: An ancient spiritual geometric symbol or diagram used for connection with the self and the universe

mantra: A sacred word or sound used to aid meditation and connect with the higher realms

mental body: The fourth body within the seven bodies of humans, made of thoughts

mudra: A symbolic hand gesture or body pose of power, used in yoga during *pranayama* or meditation

nadi: Energy channel or pathway where *prana* flows

Nadi Shodhana: A breathing technique to cleanse and purify the subtle channels; also known as alternate-nostril breathing (*Nadi* = channel; *Shodhana*= purification)

Nirvana: The ultimate state of liberation and release from the repeating birth, life and death cycle; freedom, happiness

nirvanic body: The seventh and last subtle body of humans; the container of all subtle bodies

physical body: The food body, made up of matter and five elements: bones, muscles, organs, fluids and water

prana: Life-force energy

prana shakti: Cosmic life force

pranayama: Control of the breath/*prana*

Purusha: A cosmic being or self of pure consciousness

Reiki: A Japanese spiritual practice that generally involves channelling universal life-force energy through the hands and symbols

sadhana: Daily spiritual practice

Samadhi: A state of intense concentration achieved through meditation; a final stage in yoga

shakti: The divine cosmic feminine energy

Shaktism: A branch of Hinduism that worships the Hindu goddess Shakti

Shiva: The greatest god in Hinduism; the universal consciousness force and the father of yoga

the Source: Where everything originates or can be obtained

Spirit: The soul; an eternal entity that survives the death of the physical body

spiritual body: The fifth subtle body in the seven bodies of humans; the body that represents the true self or spirit

subtle body: Energy body

Tantra: The esoteric tradition of Hinduism and Buddhism that involves a set of theories, methods, techniques and practices used in yoga

Tattva: Principle, element or truth

third eye: The sixth chakra, which connects us to the inner realms and higher consciousness; also known as Ajna

universal energy: A conscious force that animates and connects us all

Vedas: The earliest collection of Indian scriptures, consisting of hymns, methods, philosophy and guidance

yang: Masculine energy force in ancient Chinese philosophy

yantra: A sacred geometrical symbol or diagram used to aid meditation or worship of a deity in Tantric tradition

yin: Female energy force in ancient Chinese philosophy

Yoga Sutras: A collection of 196 Sanskrit truths, regarded as the authoritative text on yoga

yogi: A male practitioner of yoga

yogic: Relating to the activity or philosophy of yoga

Index

Acknowledgements

I dedicate this book to my mother, Thimela Scandella, for being the inspiration behind it – I am forever grateful for all the knowledge I learned from her; to my sisters, Alcira and Thimelvy, for always being there to support me; to my soulmate, Paul, and to my beautiful daughters, Paola and Viviana, for loving me unconditionally, just the way I am.

About the Author

Thimela Garcia is a Venezuelan-British yoga teacher, member of the Yoga Alliance and certified holistic practitioner based in London. After practising yoga for a few years, Thimela studied and certified as a RYT200 in Kundalini yoga, among other specialities in the healing arts such as Reiki, sound healing, EFT body tapping and Indian head massage. Thimela is known across the wellness industry and social media as Chakra Mama Healing and she has taken part in a wide range of wellbeing activities such as yoga festivals, holistic workshops and retreats. Her portfolio of clients and collaborations are testament to her teachings and approach.

Also Available

Godsfield Companion: Crystals
Godsfield Companion: Mindfulness
Godsfield Companion: Yoga